Charles G. Norris

Twayne's United States Authors Series

David J. Nordloh, Editor
Indiana University, Bloomington

TUSAS 445

CHARLES G. NORRIS
(1881–1945)
Photograph by Dr. Frank Norris

Charles G. Norris

By Richard Allan Davison

University of Delaware

Twayne Publishers · Boston

Charles G. Norris

Richard Allan Davison

Copyright © 1983 by G. K. Hall & Company
All Rights Reserved
Published by Twayne Publishers
A Division of G. K. Hall & Company
70 Lincoln Street
Boston, Massachusetts 02111

Book Production by Marne B. Sultz

Book Design by Barbara Anderson

Printed on permanent/durable acid-free
paper and bound in the United States of
America.

**Library of Congress Cataloging in
Publication Data**

Davidson, Richard Allan.
Charles G. Norris.

(Twayne's United States authors series ; TUSAS 445)
Bibliography: p. 145
Includes index.
1. Norris, Charles Gilman, 1881-1945—Criticism and
interpretation. I. Title. II. Series.

PS3527.0485Z63 1983 813'.52 83-6118
ISBN 0-8057-7404-1

To Harry Phillips Davison and Alta Chalmers Davison

Contents

About the Author

Richard Allan Davison, professor of English and American literature at the University of Delaware, received his B.A. degree from Middlebury College, his M.A. degree from the University of Rochester, and his Ph.D. from the University of Wisconsin.

Professor Davison has published over forty articles on such figures as John Webster, Hawthorne, Melville, Whitman, Stephen Crane, Hart Crane, F. Scott Fitzgerald, Hemingway, Robert Penn Warren, John Steinbeck, Edward Albee, and J. D. Salinger, as well as Frank and Charles Norris, in such journals as *Modern Fiction Studies, Studies in Short Fiction, Modern Drama, Journal of Modern Literature, American Literary Realism,* and *American Literature.* His *Studies in the Octopus,* published by Charles E. Merrill, appeared in 1969. He is writing books on Frank Norris and the Norris family.

He was director of the Department of English graduate program at Seattle University and was associate chairman of the Department of English at the University of Delaware from 1969 to 1974. In Seattle he wrote and hosted forty shows in a television series entitled *Literature and Life.*

Professor Davison lives with his wife (Milena) and three children (Heather, Gregory, and Anne) in Newark, Delaware.

Preface

This book on Charles G. Norris is a pioneering effort. There are no other books on Norris. The neglect of Norris since his death parallels the attention drawn away from him during his lifetime by his brother, Frank Norris, a more talented writer and a literary genius, and his wife, Kathleen Norris, a more popular and prolific writer.

Yet he published eleven novels, many of which were best-sellers, most of which drew praise, sometimes high praise, from such writers as Theodore Dreiser, Sinclair Lewis, F. Scott Fitzgerald, J. Phillips Oppenheim, Fannie Hurst, and Edna Ferber. Norris claimed as friends or close acquaintances dozens of prominent and influential literary, theatrical, and political figures, including Alexander Woollcott, Alice Duer Miller, Dorothy Parker, Ida Tarbell, John S. Phillips, Frances Hodgson Burnett, Peter Finley Dunne, Jack Reed, Frank Doubleday, Robert Benchley, Sinclair Lewis, Fannie Hurst, Edna Ferber, F. Scott Fitzgerald, Noel Coward, Douglas Fairbanks, Mary Pickford, Harpo Marx, Theodore Roosevelt, Jr., Herbert Hoover, and Charles Lindbergh. He corresponded with Theodore Dreiser and Philip Wylie and had close family connections with William Rose Benét and Stephen Vincent Benét. In his advocacy for his brother, his wife, himself, and numerous young writers, he influenced the publishers and editors of most of the important magazines in New York City.

His relations with national and international figures, his activities as a literary agent and businessman and clubman, as well as a national and international traveler, offer useful insights into the social, political, economic, and literary scenes between 1910 and 1945. But the most important reason for studying Charles G. Norris rests on the eleven novels he wrote with dogged determination and filled with unflinching integrity. His perceptive encounters with the key issues of his day partake of the force and directness of his titles. His writings provoked the kind of critical response that reveals as much about the reviewers and their times as it does about the novels themselves.

Even his first novel, *The Amateur,* offers probing insights into commercial art and the publishing world in New York City at the turn of the century. With *Salt, Brass, Bread, Pig Iron, Zelda Marsh, Seed, Zest, Hands, Bricks without Straw,* and *Flint,* Norris tackles the weaknesses of American educational systems and the corruption in American advertising and big business. He delves exhaustively into such issues as business ethics, divorce, marriage and the business career, the career woman, birth control, the creative artist's dilemma, and national and international politics.

Charles G. Norris was a man of indefatigable energy, monumental generosity, and considerable talent for business and the arts. The extent to which he channels these energies into his fiction warrants this introductory attempt to rescue him from the undue scholarly and critical neglect that has been his for almost forty years.

Richard Allan Davison

University of Delaware

Acknowledgments

For their help I would like to thank C. Edmunds Allen, Rita Beasley, James Benét, C. L. Cassell, Alison Chandler, Malcolm Cowley, Helen Cravens, Kenneth L. Culver, Jennifer Dawson, J. William Dawson, Rosemary Benét Dawson, Ruth Dawson, Marion Dennick, Helen T. Dreyfus, Virginia Gibbons, Marsha Glassman, Ruth Gordon, James D. Hart, Hildegarde, Pyke Johnson, Jr., James Kantor, Eva Le Gallienne, Russell Lee, Elizabeth Leonard, Oscar Lewis, Deborah Lyall, Archibald MacLeish, Maria Marin, Ernest Marchand, Nancy Milford, Judith Morse, Lillian Otsuka, Theresa Peter, Mrs. C. Grove Smith, Anna Sosenko, Deborah Taylor, Anita Summer, Joseph A. Thompson, Susanne Vergara, and Franklin Walker.

My thanks to Ted Billy and Edward R. Rosenberry for their perceptive suggestions. My deepest thanks to my wife, Milena, for her patience and humor and for her invaluable suggestions throughout the writing of the book and during the living with it.

Special thanks to Dr. and Mrs. Frank Norris who spent many hours with me sharing their memories of Charles G. Norris and giving me access to, and permission to quote from, all of their family papers and documents relevant to Dr. Norris's father and mother.

I would also like to thank the Firestone Library at Princeton and the Bancroft Library at Berkeley for permission to quote from their Fitzgerald and Norris materials.

This book was made possible in part by a research grant from the University of Delaware.

Chronology

1881   Charles Gilman Norris born on 23 April in Chicago, Illinois.

1884   B. F. Norris moves his family (then including his wife, Gertrude Doggett Norris, and his sons, Frank, Lester, and Charles) to San Francisco.

1887–1888   Lester dies. The Norris family accompany Frank to Paris where he enrolls in art school.

1894   Charles's and Frank's parents divorce. Gertrude and Charles move to Cambridge where Frank studies writing with Lewis E. Gates.

1899   Charles graduates from Lowell High School and enters Berkeley as a history major. Joins Frank's fraternity, Phi Gamma Delta.

1900   Charles's father dies and leaves them no inheritance.

1902   25 October, Frank Norris dies of peritonitis.

1903   Charles graduates from Berkeley with a bachelor of letters degree in history. Takes a job with *Country Life in America* in New York City.

1905   Returns to San Francisco as circulation manager of *Sunset Magazine.*

1908   3 March, meets Kathleen Thompson. September, art editor of the *American Magazine* in New York City.

1909   Charles edits Frank Norris's *The Third Circle.* 30 April, Charles and Kathleen marry at St. Paul's in New York City.

1910   2 November, Frank Norris II born.

1911   Charles engineers the publication of Kathleen's *Mother* for the *American Magazine.*

1912   Moves with family to "Greenblinds" in Port Washington, Long Island. Charles starts work on *The Christian Herald.*

1914 Promotes the publication of Frank's *Vandover and the Brute.*

1916 *The Amateur.*

1917 May, enlists in the army. Assigned to Camp Dix, New Jersey, as captain of infantry.

1918 August, promoted to major. December, resigns from army. *Salt.*

1919 17 August, Gertrude Norris dies, prompting their return to San Francisco.

1920 April, corresponds with and meets F. Scott Fitzgerald. Makes permanent move to California.

1921 *Brass.*

1922 May, Warner Brothers purchase film rights to *Brass. The Rout of the Philistines, A Forest Play* performed at the Bohemian Club grove.

1923 *Bread.*

1925 *Pig Iron.*

1927 August, *Zelda Marsh.*

1929 3 August, *A Gest of Robin Hood* performed at the Bohemian grove.

1930 *Seed.*

1931 *Seed* filmed by Universal Pictures Corporation.

1933 *Zest.* Universal Picture Corporation buys film rights for $17,500.

1935 Kathleen's fiftieth book *(Woman in Love).* Charles's ninth novel *(Hands).*

1938 *Bricks without Straw.*

1944 *Flint,* eleventh and last novel. June, Charles has stroke in New York City.

1945 25 July, Norris dies in Palo Alto of another stroke.

1966 Kathleen dies in San Francisco.

Chapter One
Biography
Childhood

When Gertrude Doggett Norris[1] was told she had given birth to her fifth child and third son she was not enthusiastic. She had hoped that, if another child was born, it would be a daughter to replace the two girls she had lost years earlier but still mourned.[2] Exhausted after a difficult labor and indifferent to the result, she offhandedly named her son after her attending physician, Charles Gilman Smith.[3] Although the "Smith" was eventually dropped, the resulting insecurity surrounding an unwanted child haunted Charles Gilman Norris for the rest of his life, and he worked hard to ingratiate himself to others. Loving such nicknames as "Poobah," he remained especially vulnerable to affection, which helped sustain him during his fifties and sixties and especially the year he struggled to recover from the stroke that eventually led to his death on 24 July 1945.

After his birth on 23 April 1881, Gertrude continued to dote on Charles's two other brothers, Frank (eleven) and Lester (five), with an intensity she never felt for Charles. Upon Lester's sudden death (10 June 1887), Gertrude, shocked by the loss of her favored son to diphtheria, lamented that Charles had not died in his stead. Charles later recalled to his family that Gertrude had assured him that no one would ever love him. She focused virtually all her attention on the remaining older son until Frank's own abrupt death in 1902. Only then did she begin to pay a reluctant attention to her last child, born of her middle years.

Added to Charles's keen sense of maternal neglect was the desertion of B. F. Norris, who left San Francisco for a trip around the world in 1892, never to return. Gertrude obtained a divorce from him in 1894, but her bitterness over his abandonment was visited on her sons. She fought both of their marriages, initially rejecting her daughters-in-law as neither good enough for her sons nor socially acceptable to herself. When B. F. Norris died (in 1900), he left his entire estate to his second wife and his new family in Chicago. Frank and Charles had already been jolted by the sudden shift from the status of a wealthy and prominent San Francisco family to that of one living on alimony payments, although Gertrude fought success- fully (for the most part) to maintain their social standing. The shock of sudden financial reversal can be seen throughout the novels of both brothers. A scrupulous concern for money permeates most of their fiction.

When asked what was the best preparation for a writer, Ernest Hemingway replied, "An unhappy childhood." A pains- taking and conscientious researcher who spent long months, sometimes over a year, preparing for each of his eleven novels, Charles drew frequently from a reservoir of childhood rejec- tion in the creation of his most memorable characters.

Family Backgrounds

While teaching at a young ladies' seminary in Charleston, South Carolina, Samuel Wales Doggett (9 July 1800–27 August 1872), married one of his pupils, Harriet Walton (2 April 1804–7 February 1892). Upon inheriting the Doggett farm, Samuel moved with his wife back to Massachusetts, where in Mendon Gertrude and her eight brothers and sisters were born. A growing devotion to literature prompted Gertrude to follow her older brother Theophilus to teach (at sixteen) in a private school he had started near Chicago. There she thrived as an instructor, capitalizing on her quick intelligence and dramatic abilities. When her brother was killed (at the battle of Shiloh) during the Civil War, the private school was disbanded. The chaos of the war jeopardized the family holdings, prompting a courageous Gertrude to strike out alone as a teacher in the Chicago public schools. It was during this period that she studied for the stage, taking small parts, which included the role of Emilia in *Othello* in her debut at the McVicker's Theatre in Chicago.

At the time when Gertrude was beginning what might have been a highly successful theatrical career, a persistent young man, who had the means to back up his promises of matrimoni-

al security, met and wooed her. Although B. F. Norris must
have been enchanted by the young Gertrude's dramatic abilities
and later delighted in her readings to him from Dickens, his
concerns always leaned more heavily toward business than the
arts. He urged both Frank and Charles to follow him in his
world of business and finance. Frank failed him in both aptitude
and interest. Although Charles did follow his brother into a
writing career, B. F. Norris would have been proud of his
youngest son's business acumen.

Benjamin Franklin Norris, Sr., was born in central Michigan
to the hard life of a farmer's son. Lameness from a hip disease
prompted an exchange of the physical rigors of the farm for the
intellectual challenge of a boarding school. The fourteen-year-
old Benjamin never accepted this challenge. The attraction of a
jewelry store window display led to his apprenticeship, and
within two years he was on the road as a traveling jewelry
salesman. After saving enough money from a job with a second
firm, he started the business that gave him the confidence and
financial security to pursue and win Gertrude.[4] She was not
unmindful of the benefits available to the wife of a man already
on his way to considerable wealth. She persistently reminded
him, however, that she regretted having sacrificed a stage career
for marriage and motherhood.

Travel and Hero Worship

By the time Charles was one year old his father could afford to buy a huge house and appoint it with furniture and
art work he and Gertrude had gathered during a European
tour.

Ever restless, B. F. Norris moved his growing family west in
1884. It was the spectacular beauty of the hills and bay of San
Francisco, not the flat plains of Chicago, that accompanied
Charles's earliest memories. Unlike Frank he had no visual
memory of the Chicago that awed Dreiser's Carrie Meeber in
August of 1889. Nor did he have the Midwest experiences his
good friend Sinclair Lewis was to harness in *Main Street* and
Babbitt.

Although Charles was slighted by his mother and somewhat
overlooked by his father, his childhood was hardly one of total
rejection. His elder brother saw to that. For while Frank was

decidedly Gertrude's favorite, and although his mother encouraged him in his drawing, painting, and writing, the number one son gave little pleasure to his father by pursuing these endeavors. Reluctantly, Mr. Norris allowed Frank to turn from business studies to prepare for an artist's career in Paris. He supported Frank's wishes, however, to the extent of shepherding the whole Norris family to Europe and living there with Frank for a year before taking Gertrude and Charles back to America and reluctantly leaving the fledgling artist in Paris. But within a year (in 1889), B. F. had his excuse to order Frank back to San Francisco. His son had been neglecting his "frivolous" art for a pastime even more frivolous, wasting time and money writing fiction. It was for Charles's amusement as well as his own that Frank provoked their father's wrath.

With Lester gone as a playmate, the six-year-old Charles had found life in Paris a lonely one. Frank took pity on his little brother, spending many hours playing soldiers with him and inventing intricate stories about their diminutive toys. Charles later recalled that Frank "loved story-telling, and his imagination knew no limitations. My earliest recollections are of the endless stories of love and chivalry that he wrote about my lead soldiers, to my never-failing enchantment and delight. . . . He would spend hours fashioning wonderful cannons out of the thick handles of his paintbrushes, and the sides of cigar boxes."[5] After Charles was back in California, Frank "began writing [his brother] a novel in which all [their] favorite characters reappeared, revolving around [Charles] whom he described as the nephew of the Duke of Burgundy. . . . It came to [Charles] in chapters, rolled up inside French newspapers to save postage."[6] When B. F. Norris happened upon one of the episodes, the author was summoned home and the novel left unfinished. That Frank had taken such pains to entertain Charles, however, epitomized the closeness that was to be shared by the two brothers the rest of Frank's life. It also fired Charles's own desire to write, prompting his first extensive literary effort, a lengthy historical novel set in the twelfth century called "In the Reign of the Grand Monarch," written when he was ten years old.

After Frank returned to San Francisco to prepare for the

entrance exam to Berkeley, Charles savoured the time his brother was able to spend with him at home. Then for the school year of 1894–95 he went East with his mother and Frank, who had enrolled at Harvard to study writing under Lewis E. Gates. The brothers remained close throughout the year, although Frank had to check the thirteen-year-old's enthusiastic violation of certain privacies. While Charles was allowed to read his brother's daily themes for English 22, Frank severely rebuked him when he discovered that Charles had also been reading in his black notebook, a combination of common-place book and diary. Charles wrote in 1914: "I . . . got soundly kicked for my impertinence, but years afterward I came upon many of these same notes in his work, amplified and clarified."[7]

Frank continued to inspire Charles's admiration when, as a twenty-five-year-old adventurer, he traveled to Capetown and Johannesburg and participated in the Boer War the winter of 1895–96. Charles excitedly followed Frank's involvement in the Spanish American War in the company of such legendary figures as Richard Harding Davis, Frederic Remington, and another boy wonder, Stephen Crane. When peritonitis took his brother at thirty-two, the twenty-one-year-old Berkeley junior was all but shattered.

For the last month or so of his life Frank, his wife Jeanette, and their new daughter Billie had lived in San Francisco, planning an ocean voyage that was never to materialize. They frequently went across the bay to visit Charles at Berkeley (once staying for a few days at the Figi house). Charles went to see Frank in the hospital shortly before his terribly sudden death. A year later (1903) he recorded his profound emotions in a moving letter to Frank's widow:

My dearest sister:
   I cannot exactly recall the date but I'm quite sure that it was about the time you will get this letter that a year ago we celebrated all together your last birthday. . . . Oh—it seems so very, very long ago and I seem to feel that we were all very different people. Surely we are not the same as those four happy persons that had dinner . . . on that day in the Poodle Dog Resteraunt [*sic*]. . . . Do you remember how

afterwards we took mama to the Sutter street cars and then the three
of us went down town, again to see the sights? . . . It's so hard to go
on and keep back the tears and try to forget. I *can't* forget. Would to
God, he were here now. . . . But my grief dwindles away to nothing-
ness when I think of the emptiness and the bareness of what I know
your life must be. Dear JB, would that I could suffer more and lessen
your great grief or in some way fill the vacant place if only with my
love. And may I presume to say that were he here today I know how
proud he'd be of his wife. . . .

If devotion, pride or love could send you with this letter some spark
of happiness on your birthday, let my heart send it and believe me
now and always until death reunites one of us with him that's gone,
your devoted brother.[8]

Jeanette Black Norris Preston was to outlive Charles; but as
long as he lived, he was devoted to her and played an active role
in looking after royalties on sales and stage and film adaptations
of Frank's writings. It was Frank, however, who remained his
most important concern, at least until he met and married
Kathleen Thompson and became her sole agent and manager.

Education

After graduating from Lowell High School, Charles enrolled
in Berkeley in the School of Social Sciences in September 1899
as a history major. Unlike Frank (who was a special student for
four years, failing to graduate because of a math deficiency)
Charles went on to receive a B.L. (bachelor of letters) degree.[9]
While at Berkeley Charles threw himself into fraternity life
almost as vigorously as had Frank, joining the same Phi Gamma
Delta. He appears faithfully in the 1901 *Blue and Gold* (the
yearbook for which Frank had earlier served as art editor).
Charles is one of only four freshmen at Berkeley quoted under
"Some Proverbs." Recorded for posterity is "C. G. Norris—'Be
not wise in thine own conceit.'" He is again quoted in 1902,
this time under "Straight Tips." "Charles Norris—'That I drew
posters—witness the poster for 'Under the Berkeley Oaks,' that
my brother is Frank Norris and that I will some day write
stories like him.'"

Charles received mostly "B's" and "A's" in history, his major
subject, far surpassing Frank's mediocre record in all but

French. Except for a "C" his freshman year in the traditional course covering what the catalog described as "the history of English literature from Beowulf to the time of Wordsworth," he received "B's" in all of his English courses. Along with a pass in etomological ecology—"the influence of economic conditions on social and political development [material he drew upon for his novels]," Charles made straight "A's" in the required two-year program in military science that Frank had so disdained some ten years before. His excellent record in military science doubtless provided the groundwork for his rapid advancement to major in the army during World War I.

A large portion of Charles's stay at Berkeley was devoted to the social side of campus and fraternity life. Although there is no record of his extracurricular activities in *The Blue and Gold*, he clearly involved himself in the usual fraternity affairs. His lifelong devotion to drama and theater led to his authorship of three Bohemian Grove plays. His enthusiasm for amateur acting thrived during these college years.

Although Charles enjoyed college life, his pleasure was muted by the deaths (one hard upon the other) of both his father and Frank. Perhaps to escape his sorrowful memories (not to mention Gertrude's dominating presence), he chose upon graduation to leave San Francisco for the East, where he accepted his first job in the New York City–based *Country Life in America*. He was to serve as an assistant editor there until 1905. In New York he worked at social as well as professional advancement and was delighted by his acceptance into the exclusive Dutch Treat Club of New York City. It was a membership that was extraordinarily important to him, as was his active involvement in the Bohemian Club of San Francisco.

New York and Back to Kathleen

The social life, the drinks in the Oak Room at the Ritz and dinners in cozy restaurants after a play or an opera, scenes he described so vividly in *The Amateur* and many of his other novels, never lost their appeal. In fact, the excitement of New York's social and theatrical life proved more attractive to the young Charles Norris than his job on *Country Life in America*, for he grew tired of covering dog shows at Madison Square

Garden and writing "Hints for Tulip Raisers" and pieces on
"Fire Risks in the Country Home." Homesick for San Francisco, he returned to the other important city in his life and
secured the job of circulation manager of the *Sunset Magazine.*

The cold, rainy, wintry day of 3 March 1908 was warmed
considerably by Charles's first meeting with Kathleen Thompson, who at twenty-eight (nine months his senior) was a
successful journalist covering the San Francisco upper social
set. In *Family Gathering,* Kathleen records her memory of the
events following their introduction: "The tall dark man then sat
beside me, told me the names of the skaters I couldn't identify,
and . . . walked with me back to the office" (70–71). She recalls
how he appeared to her during their months of courtship which
led to their wedding on 30 April 1909 less than a year later:
"[He] was a six-footer, with a smooth wave of black hair, black
eyes, and a perfect skin. He was clean-shaven at this time but
presently developed a small, sharp-pronged mustache that with
his round, boyish face soon made him a target for caricaturists at
bohemian dinners on the lower East Side. . . . I was tall too,
with a heavy mass of reddish hair never correctly dressed, and
an indifference to clothes that was to remain with me all my life
and in time cause Cigi acute concern. By today's standards we
were both overweight."[10]

Charles helped Kathleen compensate for both her weight and
fashion problems by personally taking charge of her wardrobe.
Once a year he took her to get outfitted, usually at Bergdorf
Goodman's, calling out "sheep" or "goats" to the expensive
garments paraded before them. For Kathleen's summer comfort
he would shower her with tastefully bright-colored and loose-
fitting Chinese Coolie outfits, complete with full trousers and
mandarin-collared tunics, all in expensive silks. Nor did he
neglect his own wardrobe, glorying in his well-tailored suits
made from beautiful cloth, his monogrammed shirts and expensive accessories. C. Edmunds Allen describes his in-law and
drinking companion in the last years of Charles Norris's life:

Every detail in Major Norris's dress was studied and perfect.
Usually he wore a grey fedora hat, blue or grey pin stripe suit, white
shirt, necktie in perfect taste and carried a cane with a silver top. His
mustache was waxed and his gray hair brushed back. On most persons,

this costume probably would have looked like a second class Beau Brummel. On him it looked natural and becoming.

Whenever he entered a room, his presence was felt.

Headwaiters, if they didn't know him, thought they should and gave him first class treatment.[11]

He was always a dapper dresser, to the point of vanity. And all the towels in the Norris household bore the initials CGN.

During their courtship and throughout most of their thirty-seven-year marriage, a week would not go by without some gift from Charles to Kathleen. Among the first presents that Charles gave Kathleen during the first month of their acquaintance was a jar of stuffed olives and one of Frank Norris's rings. Even before Charles had secured another job in New York City (this time it would be with the *American Magazine*) he added a proposal of marriage to his presents and suggested that they move to the city and "live there the way Frank and Jeanette did."[12] Kathleen resigned from the *San Francisco Examiner* and made the long train ride East with her fiancé's mother. Although her initial reception of this future daughter-in-law was scarcely warmer than her earlier response to Jeanette Black when Frank disclosed their engagement, Gertrude insisted on being an intimate part of the wedding. Kathleen later reported, "In the fourteen days of her stay I was her sole companion [Charles being at his office all day] and we explored the city together; every night Cigi and I dined with her, very careful not to open unsympathetic subjects to hurt her feelings. . . . And after dinner she read to us, in her hotel room . . . all of Frank Norris's *Pit* and *McTeague,* Kipling's *Boots* and *The Lay of Mary Gloucester,* and much of Noyes and Francis Thompson, and as far in Browning's *Ring and the Book* as Caponsacchi."[13]

Marriage and the Early Years as Agent

As soon as Gertrude was off for the West Coast, the newlyweds began to enjoy their newfound privacy in an old brownstone apartment on East Seventy-Sixth Street. Charles would spend his days as "man-of-all-work" on *The American,* relishing the friendship with his best man, Albert Boyden, and sharing with Kathleen the acquaintanceship of such members of the *American* staff as Ida M. Tarbell, Ray Stannard Baker, John

Siddall, Finley Peter Dunne (of "Mr. Dooley" fame), Juliet Wilbur Tompkins, Josephine Dodge Daskam, Charles Hansen Towne, Wallace and Will Irwin, Inez Haynes Gilmore, Theodosia Garrison, Franklin Pierce Adams, and Joseph Chase, the painter.

While her husband was at the office, Kathleen began to write again in her spare time. Before long she had sold "three brief sketches" to *The Evening Telegram.* When she surprised him with her version of "chicken gravy" (eighty-seven dollars in checks placed in the gravy boat), Charles was "incredulous, exultant, and then brooding."[14] From that day he became her manager, editor, and agent. He took over all these jobs brilliantly, just as he bought theater tickets, arranged cross-country and cross-world journeys, supervised what was to become a large household (including seven servants), and managed their very complicated financial affairs, all the while writing articles, short stories, plays, and his eleven lengthy novels.

During all but the first year of their married lives, the Charles Norris household was filled with children. Francis (Frank) Norris was born on 2 November 1910. He was to be their only natural child, although they adopted another son (William Rice) and raised a nephew and two nieces from childhood to marriage. In the spring of 1912 Kathleen suffered the traumatic loss of her tiny twin daughters in their infancy. The shock of their untimely deaths may have also curtailed Charles and Kathleen's sexual intimacy. Love, respect, and friendship remained, but much of their sexual passion was channeled in other directions. Kathleen became even more of a motherly and sisterly companion; he remained her aggressive promoter and devoted friend.

After the phenomenal success of Kathleen's first novel *Mother,* revised at Charles's urging, they moved to Greenblinds of Port Washington, Long Island, a house that the Sinclair Lewises later enjoyed. Charles and Kathleen also joined the Port Washington Beach Club, as did Kathleen's sister Teresa and her new husband, William Rose Benét. The Norrises continued their close relationship with the Benéts and lovingly raised the three Benét children after Teresa died and William married Elinor Wylie.

By 1912, Charles was working as assitant editor of the *Christian Herald,* the last civilian job he would hold in the employ of another. In 1914 Kathleen's industry and Charles's management allowed him to resign from the *Herald* and accelerate his efforts on behalf of both himself and other writers. In much the same way as William Dean Howells, Charles was the advocate for countless fellow artists. His main promotional efforts, however, remained in the family, as evidenced by his continued championship of Kathleen's prodigious literary output, his own novels, and his dead brother's reputation.

Convinced that Frank was a great American novelist, Charles did all he could to canonize him. His successful efforts to get *Vandover and the Brute* published posthumously (in 1914) by Doubleday is an early example of the persuasive abilities Charles coupled with an enormous knowledge of the political and logistical intricacies of the publishing world. Among the many people he successfully enlisted in his campaign for *Vandover and the Brute* was Frank's friend Theodore Dreiser. That he managed to get Doubleday to print his own first hard-covered publication is another indication of his persuasive powers. Although this slim pamphlet, *Frank Norris 1870–1902: An Intimate Sketch of the Man who was Universally Acclaimed the Greatest American Writer of His Generation,* had an uncertain effect on the sales of *Vandover and the Brute* (which was not a great commercial success), it did introduce his own name.

Charles's 21 November 1913 letter to Jeanette Black Norris is typical of the hundreds of shrewd letters he would write over the next thirty-one years concerning the machinations of the publishing world. It demonstrates his genius for detail, a knowledge of in-house politics and his unabated willingness to perform a valuable service for his brother's widow:

My Dear J.B.:

I just got your wire and have sent the contract down to Doubleday Page & Company to be made out in your name. You will find the check for a thousand dollars enclosed.

It has been much more difficult to sell "Vandover" than I imagined. I was completely unsuccessful in disposing of the serial rights. It was submitted to McClures, Cosmopolitan, Hearsts, Saturday Evening Post, Metropolitan and the American. The general feeling coincided with what Mr. Lorimer [George Horace Lorimer, editor of *Saturday Evening Post*] said in the letter I sent you. I thought it would be poor business to serialize the story in a second rate magazine, even if they would be willing to do it. I came near landing McClure's. Had I been successful I should have been able to send you $2,500! . . . I submitted the manuscript at the same time to the publishing houses, telling them it was being considered serially. . . . However, they were all afraid of it. Appleton's turned it down flat. Century would give no advance and would not consent to exempting the English rights. Stokes felt that they could not do the book justice. Of course Doubleday Page weren't aware of this. They are congratulating themselves on getting it and I think we should be glad too. I tried to get them to come through with $3,000 as an advance but they would not stand for that. But we ought to make at least the difference from the English house. My object in suggesting these terms was to force the publisher to advertise and to make it *worth his while* to advertise. Two thousand dollars advance is a royalty on 14,000 copies. They have got to sell that many to get their money back. The ten percent royalty gives them a leeway to spend money in advertising. They think they can sell 25,000 copies and I think they ought to. Maybe more! They are going to make a big splurge and make it a big spring book. Of course you know, between you and I, it is a terrible book. There is no love interest. The story's not connected and you soon lose interest in the hero, and it ends in catastrophe worse confounded. . . .

I have some great ideas for publicity in connection with the publication of the book and I think I can have a lot of attention given the book in the newspapers about the time it is published.[15]

In a letter six months later (8 May 1914) written soon after the publication of *Vandover,* a letter mainly devoted to his account of his negotiations on behalf of Jeanette for the dramatic/film rights to Frank's *The Octopus* and *The Pit,* Charles concludes that "'Vandover' seems to be going very well. The reviews are all complimentary which is a great satisfaction to me. Last week the book was fourth in New York on the list of best sellers."[16]

Charles continued to serve as Jeanette's agent and guide regarding the copyrights and film rights to his brother's works. It was the kind of magnanimous service he later performed for Charles Caldwell Dobie and Franklin Walker and countless other friends and acquaintances.[17] Excerpts from two of his affectionate letters to Jeanette regarding business affairs again speak for themselves. On 8 May 1914 he wrote: "Your telegram was a joy and brought great happiness to both Kathleen and myself. I know what this must mean to you and Frank

[Jeanette's second husband]. God bless all three of you!" And in the next paragraph:

> I received your Power of Attorney and enclose herewith check for $450.00. . . . Brady is under contract to produce "The Octopus" in addition to "The Pit." I do not know how soon the royalties will come in. . . . Closing the contract has been fraught with all sorts of complications. Doubleday Page & Company followed their usual penny-pinch policy. At one time Brady, D. P. & Co., and myself all threatened to sue one another. Of course that was a bluff on my part, but I didn't think it was on theirs. The one thing I wanted to keep you free from was the possibility of a suit and this I have done. . . . It would be amusing if it were not for the fact that there was so much dirty squabbling. . . .[18]

And in another (undated) letter about this same affair he wrote: "Dearest J.B.—Here's money at last! I'm glad there's something tangible to send you although it's by no means what you ought to get. Brady claims he sold 'The Pit' to the World Film Co. for $50,000,—and that 10% of that is all the royalty due D. P. & Co. and you. Thats [*sic*] $5000.00. . . . I . . . enclose D. P. & Co.'s statement and Russell Doubleday's letter. *Please return this letter to me.* I must have it for my files. . . . I love you very dearly and shall always. Don't believe that I have grossly mismanaged your affairs. *I haven't.*"[19]

Charles's letters recording the financial and political intricacies of the publishing world overwhelmingly confirm Kathleen's later admission of her good fortune to have married into a family that "knew the ropes." Without him she would never have gained the degree of popularity that made her one of the best paid writers in the world. Nor, without Charles as his advocate, is it certain that Frank Norris would have the reputation he has today. Before and after his efforts with *Vandover and the Brute,* Charles was also instrumental in the publication of editions of Frank's works and key profiles, articles, and introductions written about him. Charles's influence, involving various publishers and such literary figures as Charles Caldwell Dobie, Irvin S. Cobb, Rupert Hughes, Will Irwin, Juliet Wilbur Tompkins, Christopher Morley, H. L. Mencken, Theodore Dreiser, and F. Scott Fitzgerald (as well as prominent stage and screen figures), embraced Franklin Walker's 1932 full-length biography on Frank Norris as well as various stage and screen versions of Frank's fiction.

Agent, Author, and Officer

By early 1915, having quit his job with *The Christian Herald* to divide his time among his domestic responsibilities, his managing and editing of Kathleen's work, the furthering of his brother's and numerous acquaintances' reputations, and the launching of his own literary career, Charles was well into the writing of a novel centered around New York City. On 28 July 1915 he signed a contract[20] with George H. Doran Company of New York for the publication of this first novel, then titled *Cary Williams Amateur,* and later (in 1916) published as *The Amateur.* He also made a trip by train with Kathleen to visit California, the kind of cross-country trip that was to become an annual affair. They remained eager and proud citizens of both coasts, soon becoming enthusiastic world travelers as well. When they traveled to New York in the 1920s, 1930s, and 1940s, they would take a spacious suite at Hotel Chatham and Charles would entertain lavishly. Drinks and drinkers would flow around the teetotaling Kathleen, who appeared oblivious to the violation of both the law (until 1933) and her own antipathy to alcohol.

They were still living in Port Washington when, as Kathleen recalled, "Early in 1917 it was war . . ."[21] and Charles was rushing off to officers' training camp as a volunteer eager to encounter an enemy that he was never to encounter. Within months, however, he was graduated and assigned to the 153rd Brigade at Camp Dix, New Jersey, as captain of infantry. He remained there training troops until the war ended.[22] In August 1918, four months before the armistice, he was promoted to major, a title he was proud to use as a civilian.

Seven years earlier Kathleen's favorite sister in the extraordinarily close-knit Thompson family had married the young poet William Rose Benét. During the last year of the war Teresa and her children shared a nanny with Kathleen, her son, Frank, Jr., and her adopted son, William, and together they rented a house in Mount Holly to be near Camp Dix. Kathleen never fully recovered from Teresa's sudden death (of influenza) in January of 1919, while the Norrises were in San Francisco, unaware of her illness. Leaving the boys with Kathleen's other sister Mark, they had taken one of their cross-country train rides, she for a serious operation, he to show off his uniform to Gertrude and to his fellow Bohemian club members.

Charles, who resigned from the army in December 1918, had spent much of his spare time writing a novel. On 23 March 1918 he signed a contract, this time with E. P. Dutton, to publish later that year *Salt, or The Education of Griffith Adams.* Ignorant of Teresa's illness and sufficiently recovered from her operation, Kathleen was able to share her husband's dual excitement in the Allied victory and the publication of his novel by dancing in the New Year (1919) at the Del Monte Hotel near Monterey.

Returning to the east after Teresa's funeral, Charles and Kathleen shared their grief with her surviving sister (Mark Hartigan) and brought comfort to the three children, living with the bereaved William Rose Benét. When the Hartigans (including Mark, her husband, Happy, and their children) were sent by the navy to Rio de Janeiro, Charles and Kathleen joined them. They remained in Brazil while Charles worked on his new novel *Brass* until Gertrude Norris's death prompted their return to California in September of 1919.

When Charles was stopping over in New York the next April, he wrote to F. Scott Fitzgerald, acknowledging Fitzgerald's letter in praise of *Salt* and setting up a meeting with him.[23] The summer of that year the Norrises bought a two-hundred-and-fifty-acre ranch (La Estancia), a mountain retreat in Saratoga, California, surrounded by beautiful redwoods. And that winter "four years after the Rothenburg plan had been disrupted by the war . . . [they] made their first visit to Europe. . . ."[24]

Their stay in London included a dinner with John Murray who, representing Constable and Company, had recently sent him a royalty statement (covering the period ending 31 December 1920) concerning *The Amateur.* After Easter in Paris they renewed their acquaintanceship with Samuel Goldwyn; they had sailed to England together and now returned together to New York. During the crossings Charles further extended his professional involvements and those of Kathleen to include future Hollywood productions of their works. Goldwyn re-

mained one of their many contacts with the theatrical and film
world. That year, for instance, Charles and Kathleen went to
Culver City, where she was given a studio to herself in the
Metro-Goldwyn-Mayer plant to write movie scripts, later creating silent film vehicles for Mary Pickford.

Growing Reputation

In July of 1921, E. P. Dutton published Charles's third novel
Brass to favorable reviews by many well-known novelists (with
the exception of Fitzgerald), as well as the majority of critics.
Charles was cheered by high praise from the likes of Fannie
Hurst, H. L. Mencken, and Sinclair Lewis, for he had taken
risks in dealing liberally with the issue of divorce in a book he
subtitled *A Novel of Marriage*. To his equal delight *Brass* was in
its twenty-fourth printing before Christmas time. On 1 February 1922 he signed a memorandum of agreement with Curtis
Brown Ltd. and William Heinemann for the British edition of
Brass. In May of the same year he was perhaps even more
gratified by the Warner Brothers purchase of the film rights to
Brass.

Perhaps Norris's greatest salve to his ego in 1922 involved his
persistent attempts to compensate for his deeply felt childhood
insecurity by excelling in amateur theatricals. With the 28 July
production and ensuing publication of *The Rout of the Philistines, A Forest Play* by his revered Bohemian Club at San
Francisco that same year, he felt he had won a major skirmish in
his ongoing battle for recognition by a club that had elected
Kathleen's father to its presidency twice and had already
honored Kathleen's brother Joe with the same office.

By 14 April 1923 Charles had signed a contract, again with
E. P. Dutton, for the publication of his fourth novel in eight
years. *Bread* was published in August, "Dedicated to the
Working Women of America." Charles's even-handed descriptions of a woman's day-to-day struggle in a business world,
where equal pay for equal work was treated seriously by
virtually no one, were in many ways more controversial than
the subjects of his three previous novels. His account of a
woman's inability to be happy either as a housewife or a career
woman held up a mirror to an uncomfortable reality that he had

witnessed more pointedly in his personal involvements with magazine and publishing houses than in any accounts he had read. In his portrait of a woman who ends up a failure in both business and marriage, Charles draws no clear-cut moral, offers no model for success, despite one available in his own household. The woman closest to him seemed vibrant proof, of course, that both worlds could be conquered. Although Kathleen urged women to be full-time mothers and wives, to stay at home and rock babies and bake brownies, she was professionally mobile, making speeches and writing articles when she was not composing her novels, interrupted by nothing but a game of solitaire when there was a temporary pause in her torrent of words. Charles looked to his earlier days in business offices and outside his immediate family to find for *Bread* female models more vulnerable than the atypical one that Kathleen provided. The resulting protagonist, Jeanette Sturgis, was a composite creation that convinced and intrigued most of his reading public.

Arthur H. Jacobs of Metro Pictures Corporation thought enough of *Bread* to purchase the movie rights. That Sinclair Lewis and his wife shared the enthusiasm of many reviewers is apparent in a 28 September letter inviting Charles and Kathleen to visit them in Venice: "Bread has just come—Gracie snatched it from me—she seems to like it best of all your novels—and now I've begun it. The little I've read seems to me authoritative and extraordinarily interesting." One week later (5 October 1923) E. Phillips Oppenheim pleased Charles with his praise of an earlier novel. In a letter from England inviting the Norrises to visit them, the British author wrote: "I have just finished 'Brass' and am amazed that I have not heard of it more in this country. It seems to me such a wonderful study of the most discussed of our social institutions."[25] Charles G. Norris's reputation continued to blossom.

Established Professionals

It is remarkable, considering all he had devoted to his and Kathleen's careers during 1923 and 1924, that Charles was ready to sign a contract with E. P. Dutton (on 10 April 1925) for his fifth novel. *Pig Iron* appeared to favorable reviews the month after the April publication of *The Great Gatsby*. Charles knew that his son would appreciate the significance of the dedication of *Pig Iron* to Frank Norris II, just as he had thrilled to his brother's dedication of *The Pit* (1903) to Charles Gilman Norris over twenty years before. It is also significant that a key theme in *Pig Iron* involves the difficulties of communication between parents and children, something that Charles was to explore in his novels with deepening awareness as his gruff but kindhearted relationships with William and Frank, and Jim, Rose, and Kit Benét became increasingly complex.

By 1926, however, when the children were twenty, sixteen, twelve, eleven, and nine respectively, Charles was still quite able to deal with the logistics of a large family, which included the maintenance of both winter and summer homes in California, an apartment in New York, and private schools for five children. And he managed all of this without the abatement of his vast professional and social commitments. Representative events in the typically busy year of 1926 included his successful negotiations with Curtis Brown Ltd. and John Murray for the English edition of *Pig Iron,* the publication of a story, "John Rossiter's Wife," in the 26 June issue of *Collier's,* and the arrangement of a November dinner party (one of many he hosted and/or attended each year) at the Bohemian Club for H. L. Mencken. Charles was also hard at work on his sixth novel while managing most of the private and professional affairs of Kathleen, who continued her yearly output of roughly two and a half novels and numerous short stories and articles, along with her full schedule of speaking engagements and charity work.

Zelda Marsh was published by E. P. Dutton and Co. in August of 1927. By now Charles's reputation and bargaining skills were such that both English and German editions were also under contract for publication before the year's end. While Charles was reading proofs of *Zelda Marsh* and overseeing the annual move to their Saratoga ranch, Kathleen was fulfilling the terms of one of many contracts he had negotiated for her that year. In the Norris scrapbooks is visual evidence of this—a photo of her sitting between Douglas Fairbanks and Mary Pickford captioned "At Pickfair May 1927—Working on 'My Best Girl' 1927." Kathleen is smiling bravely despite her antipathy towards a woman who was America's golden-haired sweetheart to the world but to her an egotistical little prima donna. The money was good, helping to defray their heavy monthly expenses and adding to their nest egg.

La Abierta, Family, and Bohemia

Also in 1927 Charles supervised the design and building of their "dream house" on a spacious lot in Palo Alto adjacent to the Stanford University campus, where son Frank would visit with his fraternity brothers during the years he was a Stanford undergraduate and medical student. It is a beautiful house (now the Stanford University Newman Club Center) with meticulously designed rooms and balconies facing an inside patio and garden. Both Charles and Kathleen delighted in their winter "Abierta" dinner parties as much as they enjoyed having relatives and friends visit them during the long summers at the ranch.

Friday nights were set aside for Charles's stag poker parties. Dr. Russell Lee recalls the elaborate roast beef dinners that preceded each of these occasions. Charles would first invite the guests to sample five different red wines with masked labels. During the years that Dr. Lee knew him, it was Charles's custom to drink several highballs, imbibe much wine with his hearty prime rib dinners, and smoke three packs of cigarettes a day. Although he had one of the first outdoor pools in Saratoga, croquet (a game at which Kathleen outshone him) was too often his most strenuous exercise. The sedentary life took its toll. After administering a thorough physical exam the year before Charles's stroke, Dr. Lee advised him to take exercise (at least twenty daily laps in the pool), refrain from cocktails, limit himself to one glass of wine with dinner, and stop smoking altogether. At first incredulous, Charles absorbed the advice and then responded simply that "Life to me under such conditions would be unacceptable."[26]

Shortly after he moved his family into their new Palo Alto house, Charles's correspondence with an already close acquaintance became more frequent as their friendship blossomed. In a letter dated 30 March 1928 he congratulates Charles Caldwell Dobie on his *Mercury* article (published by H. L. Mencken) on Frank Norris, which later became the lengthiest and the most informative introduction to the ten-volume edition of the works of Frank Norris that Doubleday was to publish under Charles's guidance later that year.[27] Charles thrived on social gatherings with his fellow professionals, sharing the successes of the Norris family with open generosity. Along with a note from Charles to Dobie, typically inviting him to dinner and then to a play, is a handwritten invitation to help the Norris family celebrate Charles's forty-seventh birthday.[28]

Through 1929 and the stock market crash (which occasioned the loss of over a half million dollars of family investments— which were, under Charles's guidance, then recovered within a year)[29] many of Charles's activities continued to involve Charles Caldwell Dobie. A 21 February note regards a mutual acquaintance, the influential drama critic George Jean Nathan, and another note (dated 8 March) from Charles to Dobie requests that Dobie share a dinner with him and Kathleen in honor of their twentieth wedding anniversary. Another invitation to Dobie from Charles is to the annual Fourth of July party at their ranch in Saratoga. Fellow Bohemian Club member Dobie was in attendance that summer for the performance of Charles's *A Gest of Robin Hood*. This, Charles's second "high jinks" play, was also published by the Bohemian Club of San Francisco. A memento of the occasion of Charles's *Gest* is a Bohemian Club poster with caricatured drawings (by long-time friend and cartoonist Herbert Roth) of author Charles Norris and director Reginald Travers with "Certain People of Importance" (Kathleen's new novel) printed on the top and "Robin Hood" printed on the bottom. The energy Charles poured into his social and theatrical lives in 1929 was immense. Despite these activities, his fiction writing continued.

The "Memorandum of Agreement" for *Seed,* dated 10 April 1930, promises delivery of the "revised version" to his new publisher by 1 May. Charles had convinced Doubleday, Doran and Company, the publisher of Frank's and Kathleen's novels, to take him aboard. With the exception of *Hands* (1935) all of Charles's remaining novels would bear the Doubleday, Doran house imprint.

In Dr. and Mrs. Frank Norris's library is a first edition of *Seed* inscribed "To Alice—with love from Charles G. Norris 1930," the first formal acknowledgment of the importance of a woman who was to become Charles's and Kathleen's only daughter-in-law. Long before her 1932 marriage to Frank she would, along with his other youthful intimates, be calling him "Poobah" and providing him with an outlet for his love and affection that he enjoyed the rest of his life. As recorded in Kathleen's *Family Gathering,* an unusual variety of nicknames bespoke the warmer, more private side of a man who could send a publisher scurrying to draw up a more favorable contract or test the mettle of a child one minute late to breakfast (which he insisted be served at 8:00 every morning of the year no matter what had transpired the night before) with his booming admonition: "What do you think I'm running, a boarding house?" Kathleen fondly recalls: "It was Cigi's fortune to marry hesitantly and with foreboding, into a large clan, and by every member of which he was loved in return. This was evinced by his nicknames; no relative-in-law ever had so many. He was 'Chas' to his brother Frank, 'Doc' to Jeanette Norris, 'Chuck' to Irvin Cobb, and to James Montgomery Flagg, who did his portrait in crayons, 'Poobah' to his grandchildren, 'Maje' to Walter McLellan, his friend and secretary [and later Kathleen's] for twenty years, 'Don Carlos' to Aunt Kitty, 'Nunc' to the undergraduate body [at Stanford] and 'Cigi' to all and sundry."[30] He often signed his letters "Ceegee" and, occasionally, with or without his formal signature, on presentation copies of his books or on his photographs he wrote "Poobah." To his 1917–18 letters to Kathleen he affixed such names as Tarley, Fatso, Fatty Arbuckle, William S. Hart, and Charlie Chaplin. Those not so friendly toward him were known to call him "Charlie" and "Soggy" behind his back.

Soon after the August publication of *Seed,* his seventh novel, Charles signed a contract with Universal Picture Corporation for the film rights. He was gratified by the very substantial $15,000 check; but perhaps even more important to Charles was a 20 October letter from Theodore Dreiser. In response to the inscribed copy Charles had sent to him, Dreiser wrote: "Dear Norris: 'Seed' is a serious sociologically valuable documentation of birth control. It is a large and almost more technical than human subject and looked at in that light, I feel you have done very well with it. . . ."[31] High praise from Dreiser, this letter also marked the thirtieth anniversary of

Frank's championship of *Sister Carrie* as a reader for Doubleday, Doran. The Norris/Dreiser relationship had in a sense
come full circle.

The Brother and the Biographer

By early spring of 1931 Charles was visiting the movie set of
Seed. In one of the family scrapbooks are photographs of
Charles and John Boles (the lead actor) entitled " 'Seed' Los
Angeles March 1931" and of the entire cast and author, with
Charles standing proudly in the center of the group which
includes Raymond Hackett, Francis Dad, John Boles, Bette
Davis, and Lois Wilson. Three months later Charles had his
picture taken with some of his celebrity friends from both
coasts: Harpo Marx, Alexander Woollcott, and Harold Ross.
That summer the Bohemian Club chose Charles (at fifty) to
head the annual Grove festivity, which occasion is commemo-
rated in a cartoon of him, entitled "Chas. G. Norris Sire of Friday Night 1931." It was during this Bohemian High Jinks that
Charles took Franklin Walker to the Grove to meet the editor
of Doubleday, fellow Bohemian Dan Longwell, to smooth the
way for Doubleday's 1932 publication of what is still the only
full-length biography of Frank Norris. Charles gave much help
and encouragement to Walker throughout the project; although
some of the information he gave him was inaccurate, invented,
and suspect, most of it was reliable and valuable. Charles
patiently answered hundreds of questions, many at length, both
in personal interviews and by mail. He put at Walker's disposal
family letters and manuscripts. Charles's letters and Walker's
interview notes all reveal Charles's abiding eagerness to bolster
his brother's reputation. He read and criticized Walker's manuscript and conferred with Jeanette Preston as well as the
publishers about the project during its every critical stage.[32]

A typical note from Charles to Franklin Walker, dated 7
November 1930, reveals the cooperative yet cautious nature of
the early stage of their involvement:

It is quite Okay for you to keep the photostats a little longer. Are
you through with the pencil notes my brother made in preparation of
"The Octopus"? If you could send these to me within the next week
or two I would be obliged, as I have use for them.

Withal there is a candor in Charles's revelations concerning such matters as Frank's sexual initiations that Walker may have found too delicate to print.

On 11 February 1932 Charles wired Walker from New York City that he had "put over" his biography with Doubleday. Three weeks before (on 17 January) he had wired "publishing conditions are pretty awful but I am going to the mat for your book. . . ." A letter sent the day of Charles's success shows the extent of his involvement, his generosity:

Today I wired you as follows: HAVE PUT OVER YOUR BIOGRAPHY OF FRANK NORRIS WITH DOUBLEDAY THREE HUNDRED ADVANCED TEN PERCENT ROYALTY. THEY ARE SENDING CONTRACT TO YOU WARMEST CONGRATULATIONS.

I am very happy about this as frankly it was a tough fight. Doubleday's policy at the moment is one of strict retrenchment. . . .

I fought particularly hard to secure for you the $300.00 advance, as I very much hope you will . . . use the money to defray your expenses to New York in order to consult John S. Phillips and Tom Beer whom I have seen several times. . . . Before I leave New York I have planned to see Mr. Phillips and tell him about your work.

By 5 April Charles, now back in Palo Alto, is still helping Walker with his biography:

I have written to Mr. Phillips and Mr. Beer, as you requested. . . .

I am sorry that the bibliography is too expensive for Doubleday, Doran & Company to publish. It seems a pity. I should so much have liked to have one which was correct.

Let me know if there is anything further I can do to be of assistance.

The Family Album Grows

Throughout his trips to Hollywood and New York and his efforts on behalf of Walker and many others, Charles made steady progress on his own fiction. In a 29 January 1933 agreement with Doubleday, Doran & Company, he promised to deliver the manuscript of his eighth novel, *Zest,* "not later than March 1, 1933." And, predictably, he met the deadline. But more important to him than even his novel was the addition to the family of the woman who was to be as close to him as anyone save his son Frank and Kathleen. One of the Norrises' prize possessions is a photo of a handsome couple, Frank Norris II and Alice McCreery on their wedding day, 17 April 1932.

A series of photos in the family album shows another prized member of the Norris clan, one Charles and Kathleen felt as close to as their own child. The page of photos labeled "Mr. and Mrs. [Gerry] Hermann in Europe March 1933" is of Billie Norris and her husband. Billie was Frank's only daughter and a constant visitor at her uncle's and aunt's homes. Despair over an incurable illness prompted her to take an overdose of sleeping pills in 1942. (Within the year after her suicide her husband was to take his own life.) Charles was devastated. He felt as if his own daughter had died. Kathleen had lost, with Gerry Hermann's suicide, "her favorite croquet partner and her dear friend."[33]

The wedding of another niece, Margaret Hartigan of Shanghai, prompted Charles's and Kathleen's first world tour. On 4 October 1933 the Norrises left for Hawaii on the first leg of a "world wide" tour that took them to Europe, China, and Russia. The extended tour was well deserved, as in the spring of this busy year Charles had presided over the publication of his eighth novel *Zest,* an event leading to his 27 May contract with Universal Pictures Corporation for the film rights. The $17,500 he received from Universal is further evidence of the increasingly profitable arrangements Charles was engineering. Many of the lucrative returns on the products of his own pen were always bolstered by the considerable leverage of Kathleen's reputation. If an editor agreed to certain terms regarding his own novels, he would assure him of further benefits from the typewriter of Kathleen. Along with her greater popularity came fuller material rewards for them both, more lavish entertaining, more extended travel.

On 25 January 1934, for instance, the *American Magazine* sent "Ceegee" a "check for $25,000, this being for the *first* installment of Kathleen's *Beauty's Daughter.*" Kathleen continued to make those lucrative scriptwriting forays to Hollywood. A photo of Kathleen, Kit and Rosemary (her nieces) and Janet Gaynor is entitled "Helping Janet Gaynor Film 'Change of Heart' Fox Lot: Los Angeles: April 1934."

Some five weeks after the publication of Kathleen's fiftieth book, *Woman in Love,* Charles began formal negotiations (on 6 March 1935) with a new publisher for his new novel. Nine months later the rather complicated negotiations (during which Charles took Farrar and Rinehart to task in lengthy letters for not living up to their initial agreement) were successfully concluded in his favor through a letter written just before Christmas. Stanley M. Rinehart's compliance with Charles's detailed demands was a timely gift for Charles's favorite day, even though it was the only Christmas he would celebrate in the folds of Farrar and Rinehart.[34] For, although he had triumphed again in the business arena, after *Hands* was published that year he returned to Doubleday. Two years earlier Doubleday, on Charles's firm suggestion, had reissued *Mother,* Kathleen's all-time best seller, to renewed acclaim.

Hands, dealing as it did with three generations of a family, was appropriately dedicated "To my Granddaughter Kate Norris." But, aside from this welcome addition to the family, the activities of 1935 were not decidedly different from many of their activities over most of that decade, except for Kathleen's meeting with Hitler who, because of a mutual ancestor he greatly admired, had asked to see her. Although Kathleen was ignorant of Hitler's atrocities at the time, her visit seriously damaged her friendships with many of their New York intimates, including Edna Ferber and Fannie Hurst.[35] That year saw, along with their trip to Europe, Charles's annual involvement with High Jinks and Low Jinks at the Bohemian Grove. The subject of a Bohemian Club cartoon, Jimmy Thompson (Kathleen's younger brother), was dubbed "Sire of Low Jinks 1935."

In the fall of 1936 Charles and Kathleen returned to Europe on the *Bremen* for the coronation of King George. But, again, the most important activities of the year centered around the Bohemian Club. His third play, *Ivanhoe,* was produced at the Grove that summer and later published by his favorite club. The play was a local success. The next May the Norrises were photographed in Venice. Two months earlier (15 March 1937) publishers in Denmark had agreed on a Danish translation of *Hands,* affirming his international reputation.

Although he was no closer to the presidency of the Bohemian Club by the next summer, he was still inviting famous people to the Grove. In a scrapbook photo captioned "Bohemia Midsummer 1937" appear Theodore Roosevelt, Jr., Nelson Doubleday, "Cigi," Daniel Longwell, and his longtime friend and secretary Walter McLellan. The summer had other consolations. On 12 August Charles was conspicuously present at the marriage of Kathleen's niece, Rosemary Benét, to photographer Richard Dawson. It was Charles, not Rosemary's father, William Rose Benét, who gave the bride away. He, quite typically, absorbed the considerable expense of a very elaborate wedding, during which he took great delight as both the expansive host and "father of the bride."

Even more revealing of Charles's deep-rooted generosity is the item (dated "Christmas 1937") tucked away in a box of letters, contracts, and memorabilia in the apartment of his son and daughter-in-law. A page of his sole remaining Christmas list gives poignant evidence of the care that he put into the preparations for his favorite family holiday. Attached to the list is a note from Kathleen to their son written some years after her husband's death:

> This is just to glance at and destroy—
> He had them from 1923 on and perhaps earlier than that!
> Take him all in all we shall not look upon his like again—

On this single page Charles had written next to virtually every one of the over a hundred typed names of those to receive gifts or telegrams the specific item that he himself would purchase. The list includes every servant, and every nephew, niece, grandnephew, and grandniece. It also includes such names as Fannie Hurst, Nelson Doubleday, Ted Roosevelt, Dan Longwell, and Edna Ferber (despite their alleged altercation over Kathleen's meeting with Hitler two years before). The gifts range from boxes of candy and bathrobes to toy steam engines, pocket watches, gilt bookends, baby dolls, and Donald Duck. There is an extraordinary variety of presents, each one carefully thought out and appropriate to the taste of its recipient. It is the list of a truly thoughtful, immeasurably generous man.

The Later Years

Charles's tenth and penultimate novel was written during a period of national and international turmoil. In the preparation for and writing of *Bricks without Straw,* Charles followed his accustomed method of careful research, which enabled him to give both sides of sensitive issues with the kind of scrupulous care he had given to divorce in *Brass* and birth control in *Seed.* His field research for the politically volatile *Bricks without Straw* included dinner with the controversial union organizer Harry Bridges at the Bohemian Club. Dr. Norris thinks that Bridges's presence in this inner sanctum of conservatism so outraged less liberal members that they blackballed Charles from the club presidency, sending him into a deep depression.

Around the time of the 30 March 1938 memorandum of agreement with Doubleday and Company to publish *Bricks without Straw,* the Doubleday lawyers warned Charles that some of the material could be considered libelous. Charles met with them and offered to pay any court costs out of his own pocket so long as the novel appeared unexpurgated. There was, in fact, talk of a lawsuit by Earl Warren, then district attorney with sights on the presidency of the United States. The rumored lawsuit came to nothing as Warren apparently backed off. Charles clearly and typically took many of the details in the novel from current events. The general strike in San Francisco which he depicted so vividly in his novel was real enough to prompt him in 1934 to lay up three months of provisions at the ranch against a prolonged stalemate.

Charles's assurances regarding the costs of litigation from potential lawsuits convinced Doubleday to honor their contract. The novel appeared on schedule, causing a great stir in the political circles of California. According to Rosemary Benét Dawson, the Norris/Benét family members pored over their copies of the novel trying to recognize themselves and each other in the large cast of characters. The unusual dedication certainly encouraged them in their suspicions that creativity begins with home models. Charles names all of the younger generation of the immediate family: "To Frank and Billy, Jim, Rosemary and Kit, Joey and Kath, Babbie and David, Bunga and Con, Josephine, Jane and Peggy, This Book is Gratefully

and Affectionately Dedicated." In a May letter to Walter
McLellan three months earlier there is mention of film rights to
a novel yet to be tested by public response.

While much of the post-publication stir continued at home,
Charles and Kathleen took off again for New York and Europe.
Nor were their annual festivities at the ranch disturbed. That
summer the newly wedded Dawsons recorded activities typical
of those the family had observed for a decade and a half.
Kathleen has captioned two photos: "Writing and Photograph-
ing 'A Weekend Condition 1938' Rosemary Richard" and "The
Dawsons Produce a Movie." Their film recorded what was to be
the last relatively peaceful summer among the redwoods.
Kathleen recalls in *Family Gathering:* "We were at the ranch in
the fateful August when war broke out in Europe."[36] Although
she and Charles were on opposing sides regarding America's
stance in the hostilities (until Pearl Harbor she advocated an
isolationist policy; he was pugnaciously for intervention), during much of 1939, as far as their professional and social lives
were concerned, it was business as usual. And during the late
1930s and early 1940s, Kathleen continued to write as prolifi-
cally as before and her husband/agent/manager continued to sell
her work for the highest prices.

A 31 January 1939 telegram to Charles Caldwell Dobie
regarding a luncheon Charles was having for Somerset
Maugham and numerous photos of Charles and Kathleen at San
Francisco's World's Fair record more of their typical activities
during that first war year. And two documents in the family
papers record Charles's continued involvement in the furthering of his brother's reputation. A 2 February 1939 letter
from Charles Norris to Charles Caldwell Dobie concerns the
dramatic rights to *McTeague.* A photo dated "July 1939,"
captioned " 'McTeague' dramatized by C.C.D.," shows the cast
posed on and in front of a stage with both Charles and director
Dobie. Later that year the last extant family photo during
Charles's lifetime shows the large and handsome Norris clan
posed at La Casa Abierta in Palo Alto during a break in the
Christmas festivities. By the next Christmas, most of the young
men were in uniform.

During those early war years Kathleen worked for Robert
Taft and then Wendell Willkie, speaking along with Taft and

Charles Lindbergh to an overflow crowd at the memorable Madison Square Garden rally against America's intervention in foreign wars. Although Charles supported Roosevelt's interventionist policies just as vigorously, he respected Kathleen's views and both Norrises maintained a respectful friendship with the Lindberghs, inviting them to the ranch during June of 1941. In the late summer and fall of that year feasts and games at the Palo Alto house provided a partial buffer to the news of sinking ships and burning airplanes. In August someone took a candid picture of a surfeited but contemplative Charles at the dinner table in Palo Alto, a large platter before him with the remains of the roast of beef he relished so much. It is perhaps the last recorded meal he would enjoy in such relative peace.

By 1942 Charles was hard at work on what was to be his last completed novel, still without a break in his expert management of every detail of Kathleen's career. On 23 April 1942 (Charles's sixty-first birthday) a letter from Percy Waxman, associate editor of *Cosmopolitan* to "Ceegee," offered $5,000 for Kathleen's *Come Back To Me Beloved,* "to be published complete in one issue."[37] Nor was their social life stifled. Guests continued to fill the guest cottages at the ranch. That summer Herbert Hoover sent Charles a note of gratitude (dated 8 August) addressed to "My dear Charlie," giving detailed directions to a "high classed" ranch in Jackson Hole. Hoover thanked him for "a glorious time yesterday."[38]

Charles continued to cultivate important people and accelerated efforts on behalf of Kathleen's career, particularly when the repetitive nature of her formula romances began to make magazine editors question their marketable future. In private conferences he cajoled, bluffed, and threatened both editors and publishers. In discussions, often resolved only after shouting matches, Charles's booming voice could be heard throughout the Chatham suite. Rosemary Benét Dawson recalls several occasions when Charles returned to her room with a sly smile and a wink after a noisy tirade and stunning victory over a defeated editor who had been shown the door.[39] The public gave added strength to his bargaining prowess as the war apparently did not destroy its enthusiasm for Kathleen's writings. If the enthusiasm slackened somewhat, Charles refused to let the uncertain times affect the price tags of either her work or his own. On 9 June 1943 William A. H. Birnie, the editor of *Woman's Home Companion,* sent a letter to the Chatham Hotel offering $10,000 apiece for two stories or a two-part serial by Kathleen. That same day a letter to "Ceegee" from Charles Colebaugh, editor of *Colliers,* offered $35,000 for serialization rights to a 90,000 to 100,000-word novel by Kathleen. And the same day the *Colliers* letter arrived, Charles signed his own contract (with Doubleday, Doran and Company) for the publication of *Flint.*

Stroke

His last novel appeared in January 1944, dedicated to his secretary of over two decades: "To my long-suffering, patient, and loyal friend, D. Walter McLellan." The trip that Charles and Kathleen made by train to New York City that spring was also to be his last. Charles suffered his stroke in the Persian room of the Plaza Hotel. C. Edmunds Allen, an eye-witness to the stroke, remembers it vividly:

Major Norris had made a reservation for two of us at the Plaza Hotel where Hildegarde was doing her act . . . with her white gloves and dainty handkerchief. . . .

On this particular evening we had a ringside table . . . and started with more scotches which we really didn't need and then his usual ritual of a very dry gibson just before partaking of the first course. She started her routine with the usual numbers, "The Last Time I Saw Paris," "The Monkeys Have Long Tails in Sambo-Ambo," "Je Vous Aime Beaucoup," and "Lily Marlene." She always had a running patter and Major Norris had a habit of interrupting and finishing off her gags. She liked to have him do it, and it always livened up the act.

By now we were drinking champagne.

Part of her routine was to ask the audience, "Is there anybody here from Oshkosh" or some other town that is supposed to inspire a laugh. Major Norris lifted up his hand to signify that he was from Oshkosh, and Hildegarde smiled at him and said, "Oh Mr. Norris, you've moved since you were here last week." With his hand in the air, he went over backwards in his chair.[44]

Allen, assuming that Charles was reacting to too much alcohol, drove him around Central Park in an open cab in hopes that fresh air would revive him before he deposited him in the Norrises' master bedroom at the Chatham. It was not until Charles missed his eight o'clock breakfast for the first time in anyone's memory that a physician was called.

Charles spent two months in a New York hospital before Kathleen was able to take him on the long train ride back to Palo Alto. In a summer 1944 letter to Alice, sandwiched between her nostalgic memories of the ranch and her charity work with the Foundlings, is a flash report on her plans for her invalided husband that suggests the severity of his condition:

whether I get any ranch in at all this year is debatable, for Nunc remains very helpless and though less bewildered is beginning to be exacting and I may not be able to go. My thoughts go no further than 13—count them, THIRTEEN days from now, when the hegira begins. It will be exciting but I think not too difficult; I mean to arm myself with one dollar bills and tip madly in every direction, stretcher carriers, ambulance drivers, porters. We will have to open the window of the train to get Cigi in. . . . We have a hotel in Chicago to rest in. . . . He raged at us when it dawned on hism [sic] the nurse was going; "he'd rather die, he'd gladly die," he kept saying. (He always speaks of himself as "he.") But now he seems reconciled.[41]

The incapacitating nature of the stroke deeply affected the whole family as Charles lingered between life and death for over a year, struggling to learn to talk again, terribly frustrated with his inability to exercise his usual control over his own life, unable to recapture his role of patriarch over the lives of others. One scarcely has to read between the lines of Dr. Harold C. Sox's letter (of 6 November 1944) to a fellow physician and friend, Frank Norris II, less than nine months before Charles's death:

I anticipate that your father will get better, although his prospects of useful betterment are pretty remote. . . . It takes a good deal of assurance to handle your dad when he is on a rampage, and the graduate nurses usually have the courage of their convictions and are able to carry on; also they don't quit in a hurry when they are castigated for nothing at all. . . . I can understand the difficulties for your mother, as your father might as well be dead as far as any real help and comfort that he could possibly give to her, and on top of that, she has this terrific responsibility which he has always carried. I see no reason why she shouldn't get away from the house fairly often, and I think it wise if she does, granting that the place will run reasonably well without her. . . . I think it makes little difference what sort of care he has as long as it is reasonably understanding. I think the decision should rest on the effect it has on your mother and household as a whole rather than on his welfare. . . .[42]

There is a poignant irony in the partial neglect Charles received, at both the beginning and the very end of his life, from those he loved most. Gertrude was too concerned with her own discomfort to see that he was properly named. Kathleen, frustrated with the long months of his difficult illness, was off indulging herself in one of her favorite games of croquet during his last hours. Nevertheless, Kathleen's tribute to him in her letters and in *Family Gathering* is a warm one which gnores the bad times, and there is a deep respect in her note to Frank attached to Charles's 1937 Christmas list. No doubt Kathleen's absence from his deathroom was prompted in part by Dr. Sox's advice and in part by her heartbreaking experience with a tenacious and irascible but pathetic invalid who seemed no worse to her on the day of his death than on those hundreds of other days of his semiparalysis. For Kathleen, although abundantly warmhearted, was also a realist and looked upon Charles's death as more of a release, more of a blessing, than a tragedy. She saw the continuous suffering of an incapacitated creature who was once a vigorous and clear-thinking man as the real tragedy. She was understandably relieved when on 25 July 1944 his death (as she wrote in *Family Gathering*) "came very quietly."[43]

Husband, Father, and Friend

One wonders if Charles's novels would have gone out of print as quickly as they did if his promotional genius had survived him. There is little doubt that if one or two people had put a fraction of the energy toward promoting Charles's novels, even keeping them before the public, that he had expended to keep alive the reputation of his brother Frank, his writings would not have remained forgotten for so long.

Even more of his energy went into the composition of his

novels. For to Charles writing was much more difficult than business and economics. Writing was much more difficult for him than it was for Kathleen, who regularly composed at her typewriter with little or no revision. Writing was also a more serious occupation to Charles. While she wrote mostly to entertain and give the world happy endings to help her audience escape their troubles for a few hours, he tried to write for posterity. Charles, much like Frank, could say with a clear conscience about most of his writing: "By God, I told them the truth." And he told it without shortcuts. Kathleen recalls in *Noon* how he would "sometimes hammer out three sentences in as many hours' hard work."[44] Later she remarked that his "was not a natural gift," recalling how "he fought his way from page to page, and sometimes made [her] blood run cold by tearing up the patient work of weeks, or even months."[45]

Charles's hard work and dedication helped him to carve out a more than respectable reputation during the second half of his life. Reviewers and critics came to take his work more seriously than Kathleen's. By the mid-1920s he had emerged from the shadow of the woman whose reputation he was so instrumental in creating. Yet a scant two weeks after his death, the *Saturday Review of Literature* spoke for most of the literary world that seemed to have quickly forgotten the results of his thirty years of hard work. Its 11 August 1944 obituary notice refers to him once again as "Charles G. Norris, husband of Kathleen and author of a half-dozen best-sellers of his own. . . ."

By the 1940s, however, Charles had been realistic and secure enough in his own literary reputation to be more amused than annoyed by such backhanded acknowledgment of his status. He had acquired a greater sense of humility about his writing that compensated in part for the vanities that clung to him regarding his personal appearance and social status. He also maintained a deep love for and devotion to his family and friends.

Two letters written about the same time reveal the private as well as the public man as he approached his sixtieth year. The first is to Joseph Henry Jackson, a friend of long-standing. This letter is quoted at length in chapter 6. The second (dated 22 October 1940), filled with gossip and news from New York, is to his son Frank. The letter goes beyond Charles's news of his own health, assessments of friends, and playfully grudging generosity and testifies to his love of, pride in, and concern for Kathleen and Frank:

> Mom is up to her neck in Willkie work,—radioing every day—national hookup. . . . from 3:15 to 3:30. . . . the checks are pouring in. . . . Mr. Willkie himself . . . was so impressed with her that *he* wants her to introduce *him* in her 15-minute program on the 29th and also on the 1st. Quite a compliment, I should say. Next Wednesday . . . Mom leaves for Chicago, radios at 2:15 there, then goes on to Cedar Rapids where at a Willkie rally Thursday (next day) night she introduces Governor Stassen. . . . Next day she flies back in time for her radio talk. She's loving it and gets more enthusiastic everyday. What would kill most women she thrives on. I think on the whole she has been very happy here this trip.

Love for his twenty-nine-year-old son radiates throughout Charles's rambling record of parental activities: "Dearest Mouse: I have just finished your letter and am glowing inside. . . . I have just reread your letter—and will now destroy it. How *well* you *write!* You have a natural gift of expression which I truly envy you. This is not b—s—! . . . I'd like to keep it in some safe, hidden place. With others from you. But I think it is more of a value for you to feel with absolute confidence that when you write to me, no other eyes will ever see your pages. (The pieces torn in bits now lie in the waste-paper basket!)" Eager for a swift reunion he closes with "We leave on Nov 1st; home the morning of the 4th—Monday. We'll miss your birthday [2 November] but will celebrate it on the week-end following—if you are free. The delay in our return is due to Mom's radio engagement. They want her to radio right up to the last day. . . . My love to your three girls [Allie, Kate and Nellie], to 2-ton, and my heart at *your* feet. Dad."[46]

Chapter Two
The Amateur and *Salt*

The Amateur: Story and Origin

Carey Williams, having won first prize in the state fair art contest, leaves his Midwestern town and his mother for the big test of his creative abilities and settles in New York City. Lonely, alienated, homesick, he experiences rejection after rejection from magazines, publishing houses, and advertising art departments that assault his hopes of becoming a successful illustrator. He makes friends with fellow roominghouse boarder Jerry Hart, who offers him solace in city night spots, where they spend carefree hours indulging their senses. For a time Carey is vaguely content, supporting his self-indulgence by drawing monograms for cigarette packages for "one of the smaller advertising agencies." Then Jerry Hart seduces and deserts the virginal model and Sunday school teacher Anna Blanchard, whom Carey has secretly desired. The shock of discovering her dead body ("In the last flicker of the match, he had seen her where she hung from the top hinge of the door, the congested face and the staring eye-balls on a level with his own")[1] is shattering. It is compounded by her father's conviction that Carey was her seducer.

The death of his own father, Virgil Williams (who had married Carey's mother when she was barely out of her teens and twenty years his junior, and then left her for another woman) prompts Carey's dutiful return home. Carey's memories of his father include neither deep bitterness nor strong affection. His father's enthusiasm for art and music (not shared by Mrs. Williams) was offset by the agonies of his chronic headaches.

When Carey returns to New York it is to a new studio apartment (paid for with his father's legacy), new friends (Fleming Springer, artist, and Cecilia Shaughnessy, neophyte model), and a new enthusiasm for his art. Springer, a handsome playboy with an actress (Myra) for a mistress, becomes Carey's new tutor in revelry. By capitalizing on a technique involving a special blend of white paint applied to strawboard, Carey begins to sell his reproductions of Cecilia's face wreathed by her distinctive red hair. Hung over from a drunken evening, he makes a clumsy pass at Cecilia, driving her into Springer's arms. Carey has a brief affair with Myra.

On his second return to New York, after his mother's prolonged illness and death, he discovers his illustrations on the covers of six magazines in one week. He moves into a more expensive apartment and assumes a more extravagant life-style. At the height of one of Carey's drunken sprees Anna's father shoots him, sending him to the hospital. During his convalescence a former acquaintance, Jane Boardman, initiates a courtship which leads to their marriage.

He gives up his exploitive illustrations, which are no longer unique, and takes a job retouching photographs until Jane sells his more imaginative drawing of their child. The novel ends happily with a reformed Carey beginning a successful career doing the kind of genuine art work that had always been his dream.

In the typed manuscript of Charles Norris's "My Wife" are two and a half pages that were edited out of what became the introduction to Doubleday's 1935 edition of *Mother*. One of the deleted pages contains Norris's account of the genesis of *The Amateur:*

During all this time [1908–14] I had been holding down a magazine job. I don't think I worried much about getting busy with my own pen. The urge to write was still in me, but I was putting all my spare energy into promoting my wife's success. . . . And then one day I met with a rude awakening. . . . An acquaintance introduced me to a friend as "Mister Kathleen Norris."!!!!

I shall never forget the jolt of that. It set me . . . thinking hard. All the grave doubts and fears and self questionings which Kathleen had known five years before now became mine. . . .

So I resigned my job and together, Kathleen and I, went to California and there . . . I set myself down with a block of paper, a pen and a bottle of ink and went to work. The result at the end of six months was a novel—a very indifferent one, and a year later, Mr. George H. Doran, upon the generous recommendation of my friend

Sinclair Lewis—at that time [one] of the readers for that publishing house—signed a contract to publish it. . . . it was my beginning— thanks to "Red" Lewis.[2]

Reception

The Amateur was well received for a first novel. The most unfavorable notice is a mere squib by Wilson Follett in *Atlantic Monthly* seeing in *The Amateur* "the failure to correlate the story with the artist as an artist, however sufficient he may be as a person."[3] The *New York Times* disagreed, declaring that "the vital interest centers in the character of Carey—a character very well depicted."[4] The *Boston Evening Transcript* found him "likable" as well as real and admired the original "graphic pictures of realities . . . actual happenings described with visual power."[5] The *Times* points to "what is . . . the most interesting part of the book—Carey's wanderings from one magazine to another, from one publisher to another, from one advertising agency to another in search of employment." To the *Transcript* "Every character is essential to the progress of . . . the story." And according to the *Literary Digest,* "Even if this author were not the brother of the late Frank Norris . . . he would still be worthy of reading for his descriptive work and his graphic pictures of the 'art editor.'"[6]

Pasted in the back of a scrapbook that Charles and Kathleen filled mostly with reviews and articles concerning *Brass* are over a dozen brief, but telling, British reviews of the 1920 Constable edition of *The Amateur*. Several of the British papers (including the *Times)* assumed that this was Charles's second novel, free of some of the problems of a first novel. The London *Evening Standard* found it as "engrossing as his earlier book, 'Salt' . . . far above the many mediocre novels America sends us."[7] The *Times Literary Supplement* hailed Norris's "new story [which] like its powerful predecessor, 'Salt', [is] strong in design, tense with prophetic sincerity and ruthless in its disregard of weaknesses. . . ."[8] *The Observer* waxed even more eloquent: "Mr. Norris is one of the most noteworthy of . . . diligent realists. The school includes in America . . . Theodore Dreiser, and . . . Frank Norris. . . . Mr. Charles Norris is a far more independent novelist than any of these."[9]

Although the British responses tended to overvalue *The Amateur,* even the cooler American reviews did not reflect Norris's view that his "six months" of writing had produced "a very indifferent" book.

Assessment Today

On rereading, *The Amateur* remains a very respectable performance. Norris had some trouble integrating his literary sources, but he is in full command when he is portraying the workings of the magazine art industry in New York City. At twenty-three Carey Williams is scarcely older than Norris was when he himself experienced the mixture of exhilaration and anxiety of life in New York, an only son hundreds of miles from home and mother. Carey's ambivalent reactions to his parents are clearly embellishments of Charles's own mixed feelings toward B. F. Norris and Gertrude.

Carey's father took his trip around the world when his son was the same age as Charles was when B. F. Norris took his world tour, also never to return. There are strong parallels in the young men's reactions to the deaths of their absentee fathers. Like Frank Norris and Jeanette Black, Carey and Jane are married in a simple ceremony at St. George's in New York City. Jane's surprise check for the sale of Carey's drawing is like Kathleen's surprise check (her "chicken gravy") presented to Charles on Christmas Eve of 1909 for the sale of her sketches. Carey's illustrations appear simultaneously in various magazines as dramatically as did Kathleen's early stories. And one of Carey's remarks to Jerry Hart is almost a direct quotation of Kathleen's oft-quoted sentiments: "From all inordinate and obnoxious bores, from all vainglorious and conceited asses, from all recounters of dramatic plots deliver us" (99).

It is no less surprising to find in *The Amateur* strong echoes of Frank Norris's work, notably *Vandover and the Brute* which Charles had edited for its 1914 publication two years earlier. Details of Carey's preference for a comfortable rather than functional art studio and his confused emotional response to sexual arousal are almost exactly those of Vandover. Both young artists are negatively affected in similar ways by alcohol and prostitutes. Although Carey, unlike Vandover, achieves a temporary success with his art, they are both reduced to compromise: Vandover with his enamels, Carey with his monograms. Both men are sensuously aware of their deceased fathers, Vandover by the odor of hair oil on "the governor's" abandoned hat, Carey by the odor that clings to the clothing Mr. Williams has bequeathed to him. Although, unlike Vandover, Carey ultimately triumphs, he, very like Vandover, first deteriorates emotionally and physically, moves to more penurious quarters, and approaches moral and spiritual bankruptcy at the inexorable pace of his dwindling bank account. A key symptom of the state of each is the inability to draw effectively.

Clearly the most successful parts of the novel are the scenes of New York City of the early 1900s. Norris describes from firsthand experience restaurants, bars, theaters, beaches, artists' studios, apartments, hangouts, and clubs. He recounts intriguing anecdotes about successful artists and illustrators of the day and gives detailed descriptions of their artistic techniques. Carey's frustration and discouragement as he is turned down by one magazine after another are real, as is his exhilaration over the sale of his first illustration. His struggles to come to terms with his artistic talent are firmly linked to his uncertain existence as a social animal. His joy in the camaraderie of young men out for an evening on the town is well balanced by his sense of guilt the morning after what has turned into a drunken revel.

It is in Norris's attempt to make Carey's remorse convincing that he is weakest. Nor does Carey's deep sense of responsibility for the suicide of a girl he himself had not seduced quite ring true. The omniscient author rather prudishly adds: "Carey's amusements were not of a vicious order. Women played no part in his scheme of pleasure. . . . he was singularly cleanminded, though he had no particular moral convictions on such matters" (91). But if Carey's often misplaced guilt is not totally convincing, it is at least carefully prepared for by flashbacks to the insecurities and traumas of his childhood:

Once the boy had come home late, and had entered the house not knowing his father had returned before him, carried up to bed, blind with pain. Carey romped through the hall, flung his school books into the hall closet, banged the door, and came up the stairs two at a time.

He never forgot the towering figure, clad in the white, scant night-gown, that met him at the head of the stairs. The hollow sockets beneath the contracted brows in which his father's eyes leaped as tiny flames, the drawn cheeks, the dripping grey hair, the clawlike hands, one caught at the opening of the nightshirt, the other clutching the ice cloth, and his mother's shrinking figure cowering behind, left an ineradicable impression upon his mind. The utter terror that possessed him at the moment forever left its mark upon him. (25)

The novel's essentially tight structure is an early tribute to Norris's craftsmanship. Just as early incidents prepare for later ones, there is little of the padding found so often in first novels. Jerry's seduction of Anna is prepared for by his pleasures as the boardinghouse Peeping Tom. Even Blanchard's shooting of Carey is less melodramatic than it seems in summary. It is the act of a man who believes that a seducer, a virtual murderer, of his daughter will continue to taunt him with impunity. Carey Williams seems Evil Incarnate to this befuddled father of a Sunday school teacher. Carey's own state of mind the day he is released from the hospital is similarly confused. The world he sees has the same aura of determinism Charles had noticed in Crane, Dreiser, and Frank Norris's *The Octopus* and *The Pit.*

Everything appeared new and strange to him. . . . Each of the people he gazed out upon was hurrying by, intent to fulfil a purpose, a petty, trivial purpose. . . . They all appeared ridiculous to him, running about like aimless bugs. He had touched Death's finger tips across the threshold of Life. One glimpse of that stern, grim visage had swept the cobwebs, the murk and dirt from before his eyes, and he was able to *see* now, while the poor fools he watched from the cab's window ran about in blind circles. The buildings . . . that had impressed him when first he came to the city as evidences of achievement, of romance, of power,—now were excrescences, the puny monuments of pigmy creatures that could be swept away in the winking of an eye by one manifestation of Nature. (321–22)

Despite Norris's knowledgeable writing and firm control of structure, the novel's happy ending offers too quick a solution to Carey's despair and smacks of a pandering to popular taste. After patiently editing and placing Kathleen's short stories and best-selling novels (she had six by this time), Charles knew about successful formulas and with an eye to the public's taste had made a gallant bid for his own best seller.

Salt: More Savor

Salt, or the Education of Griffith Adams covers almost thirty years of Griffith's life, beginning with his upbringing by nurse Carrie, who "frequently hurt him" and told him "that if he rumpled his dress, he would be locked in the closet." She is replaced by nurse Pauline, whose departure "after much weeping and hugging and kissing" deeply upset the seven-year-old Griffith.[10] Griffith's attractive mother, Maybelle Wagstaff Adams, alternately pets and ignores him. His father, Richard Cabot Adams, spends more time with his books than with his son, and dies in his study. Griffith is just ten and a half when his self-centered mother sends him to the Fairfield Military Academy, where he learns to study, fear, hate, lie, obey, and be alone. Only after she discovers that Griffith had been caught escaping with his only friend, David Sothern, and had been mistreated does she rescue him.

Griffith falls in love with his next teacher (Miss Fisher), who encourages him in his love of books and music. His subsequent marriage proposal prompts his mother to send him to still another institution (the Concord Family School) where, while she absents herself to Europe with her third husband, the fortune-hunting Paoli Santini, he is again baited and, after his vicious attack on one of his cruel classmates, nicknamed "biter" and "dog." Again a solitary friend aids Griffith. The wealthy Archie McCleish takes him west to Nevada for a summer of healthy ranch life. In the fall they both enroll in the University of St. Cloud and pledge (Griffith on the coattails of McCleish and David Sothern) the prestigious Delta Omega Chi. He survives the brutal initiation rites and for four years studies little, drinks much, and cheats more or less as frequently as his fraternity brothers.

Griffith's one positive intellectual and moral guide in college, the English instructor Hugh Kynnersly, who offers fine music and stimulating discussions, discovers his theft of a final exam his senior year and sees that he leaves without a degree, but not before Griffith has fallen in love with David's beautiful sister, Margaret Sothern.

His mother's death (after Santini's desertion) prompts his reunion (after fifteen years) with his half brother Leslie Wagstaff, who takes him in and gets him a job with a railroad company. There Griffith supplements his salary by cooperating illegally with Leslie's former boss and benefactor, Enos Chickering. Griffith's betrayal of Chickering loses him both his job and, for a time, his brother's sympathy and financial support. Meanwhile, Griffith has responded to Archie's marriage to Margaret Sothern by marrying Rissie Rumsford, the lower-class daughter of a fellow employee.

With David Sothern's help he gets work as a companion to Mr. Quay, a wealthy old man who sends Griffith to an austere New England mill to learn the wool business, starting him with the most menial of jobs. Rissie's death in childbirth leaves Griffith with a son, Dickie. An affectionate Swiss family nurture Dickie while Griffith renews himself in New England. Rewarded for his hard work by promotions, Griffith chooses to marry Rosa Pohli rather than the wealthy (now widowed) Margaret, who threatens to spoil his son with material excesses. The marriage promises to be a success because of positive values learned despite the contrary forces of the formal educational systems in America.

Reception

Reviewers liked *Salt* even better than they did *The Amateur*. The *London Times* (29 April 1920) ran one of the most striking and representative reviews, especially interesting since the reviewer is treating *Salt* as Norris's first novel, the British edition of *The Amateur* not appearing until months later. The *Times* praised "the distinctive quality of Salt . . . [that] can be described only by an Americanism: it has 'pep'—cogency, if one insists on a paraphrase." It sees the novel as "an indictment of the American educational system. . . . [It is interesting] to read an authoritative account of this curious and unique system as it works in a minor American university. The book makes no pretense of being lovable."[11]

The *New York Times* had already keynoted the earlier American reviews by an especially favorable assessment (16 June 1918), declaring that "As a novel it is a good story . . . as a story, it is worth reading by anyone who likes fiction of a higher grade. But it is much more than that, for the author has seriously and honestly endeavored to make it 'a criticism of life.' . . . There are many who will object to the plainness of speech. . . . But . . . they will have to admit that his purpose has been the honest one of speaking the truth." A list of the novel's targets follows, including: "irresponsible . . . selfish motherhood," the college institution which "seems almost a machine for the production of evil influences and results," the "big business corporation" whose methods "are a training in dishonesty, inefficiency, and unscrupulousness," and "the Greek letter fraternities" which exert "evil influences upon the minds, morals and standards of their members." Other newspapers picked up the *Times'* conclusion: "Mr. Norris proves . . . that his kinship to . . . Frank Norris is more than physical. For he shows in this second novel . . . not a little of the other's ability to tell a story and to envisage in its scope wide and graphic views of society and vivid character portrayals."[12] Three days later in the *Boston Evening Transcript* (19 June 1918) Edwin Francis Edgett praised the novel's "spiritual insight that does not flag," lighting up "the dark corners of human nature."[13] The *New York Call* (14 July 1918) wished this "vigorous, unusual and courageous" novel that "speaks plainly" and "with mastery" a "circulation of at least 110,000 copies. . . ."[14] The *Springfield Sunday Republican* (14 August 1918), after complaining that the title "is not related to the story," extolled the "frank realism" and "very human" depiction of lonely childhood.[15] The *New Republic* (17 August 1918) claimed that Griffith's complaint that his four years of college life were useless "would be echoed by half the undergraduates of America."[16] While objecting to "Griffith's essential flabbiness," *Bookman* (August 1918) admitted that "Mr. Norris, like Mr. Dreiser, somehow gets his effect in spite of a rather stolid and lumbering style—by virtue chiefly of his accurate and cumulative attention to detail."[17] The *Dial's* unfavorable review was exceptional, seeing "no savor in Mr. Norris's new salt," objecting to the "labored mechanical style" and the "realism" which leaves the reader what is like "a selected chamber of war horrors."[18] Although *Publisher's Weekly*

(17 August 1918) saw "not a trace of humor" and "no beauty of style except perfect clearness," it rated Norris's "powerful" novel "a beautiful piece of work as it stands."[19]

Charles G. Norris and F. Scott Fitzgerald

But of all the high praise that *Salt* received, the most ecstatic appeared over three years later amid a younger novelist's unfavorable *Bookman* review (November 1921) of Norris's third novel. Disappointed by *Brass,* F. Scott Fitzgerald recalled his stunning encounter with the earlier novel: "Although not one of the first I was certainly one of the most enthusiastic readers of Charles Norris's *Salt*—I sat up until five in the morning to finish it, stung into alertness by the booming repetition of the title phrase at the beginning of each section. In the dawn I wrote him an excited letter of praise. To me, it was utterly new and fresh and profoundly felt. . . ."[20] Three years later he wrote to Maxwell Perkins concerning *The Great Gatsby:* "My first instinct . . . was to . . . have Tom Buchanan dominate the book (I suppose he's the best character I've ever done—I think he and the brother in *Salt* [Leslie Wagstaff] and Hurst-wood in *Sister Carrie* are the three best characters in American fiction in the last twenty years . . .)."[21]

As well as adding to *Salt*'s many accolades, Fitzgerald's "excited letter of praise" of Norris's "utterly new and fresh and profoundly felt" novel began the active phase of a friendship that has gone virtually unnoticed. The Norris-Fitzgerald relationship is important for its own sake and as a springboard into a fuller understanding of a fascinating series of interconnections among writers, including Theodore Dreiser and H. L. Mencken, as well as Frank and Charles Norris and Fitzgerald, their editors and publishers. Although an extended discussion of Norris's literary milieu is beyond the scope of this book, a few details of these interconnections are essential to a fuller under-standing of him as novelist, businessman, promoter, and man. The years Charles was writing and promoting *Salt* and *Brass* were especially important in the development of all of these aspects of his career.

Fitzgerald's letter to Norris is lost but Norris's response on 18 April 1920 is worth quoting:

I was certain I saved your letter in which you were pleased to say something nice about what I had written, but some miscreant has made off with it, and I am perforce, obliged to write you care of your publishers, to tell you how very much I liked your book, "This Side of Paradise." I think it is splendidly fresh and human, and I congratulate you warmly. I wish it were possible for me to meet you for I should like mighty well to talk over some aspects of it with you. I wonder if you could take tea with me at the Ritz some afternoon next week? I am leaving for California on Friday,—the 29th.[22]

Whether they met for tea at the Ritz-Carlton Hotel is not certain, but the subsequent telegrams and letter from Charles Norris suggest that it is very likely they did meet somewhere for some literary and professional talk. In his *Ledger* for May 1920 (the month after his marriage to Zelda) Fitzgerald records ten names. One of them is "Chas. Norris."[23] The older man (Norris would have been forty at this time) undoubtedly shared with the twenty-three-year-old Fitzgerald some of the practical knowledge he had learned marketing Kathleen's works and his own. In the first of two extant telegrams[24] to Fitzgerald, from April or May 1920, Norris registers more familiarity than he does in that first letter:

HOTEL COMMODORE NEW YORK NY

FIVE PERSONS READING THIS SIDE OF PARADISE ON LAKE SHORE LIMITED TODAY   HOW DO YOU GET THAT WAY   READ CUT GLASS BOWL   GREAT YARN

The second telegram, dated 5 May 1920, radiates the kind of firm advice that one might give to a close friend. It exudes practical knowledge of the nuances of a solid business deal about which Norris had both experience and genius:

YOU WILL BE APPROACHED BY JAY PACKARD LITERARY AGENT FOR FILM RIGHTS TO THIS SIDE OF PARADISE   DON'T TAKE A CENT LESS THAN FIVE THOUSAND   REFUSE ANY ROYALTY ARRANGEMENT INSIST ON CASH PAYMENT ON SIGNING CONTRACT   DON'T LET REYNOLDS PERSUADE YOU TO ASK MORE OR TAKE LESS   GOOD LUCK

Nothing immediate seems to have come of Norris's urgings,
however. Two years later (June 1922) in a letter to Harold
Ober, Fitzgerald wrote: "The movie rights to *This Side of
Paradise* are not tied up. Several people have nibbled at
it. . . . but nothing developed."[25] In 1923 Famous Players paid
$10,000 for the movie rights, though the film was never
made.

The second letter suggests an even greater familiarity and
informality. Again I quote a previously unpublished letter:

I am a boor for not acknowledgeing [*sic*] the receipt of your volume
of Short Stories or your letter. I meant to wait before writing about
the former until I had read them all but life seems too hectic to ever
accomplish that. I like the one about the flapper who bobbed her hair
enormously.[26] Your suggestions about the special edition of my
brother's books appeals, but I fear you will not get very much
enthusiasm out of D. P. & Co. who got "stung" on an edition of
"Vandover" of 2000 copies. You might take it up with Russell
Doubleday. I'm coming on, in January, and I'll give the idea a shove
then.

I am delighted to hear you are novel-writing.[27] I make it a point *not*
to see the Post, so I do not know whether you've been slipping or not.
You can rechristen that worthy periodical "The Grave-yard of the
Genius of F. Scott Fitzgerald" if you like and go on contributing to it
until Lorimer sucks you dry and tosses you into the discard where
nobody will care to find you! I've never aspired to be a contributor to
the "Post" so I'm not speaking from personally hurt feelings.

My new novel is to be called "Brass" (lay off that title!) and it is all
done,—thank Our Heavenly Father! I don't want Dutton to publish it
until next fall. My wife says its [*sic*] better than "Salt"; I'm God-
damned if *I* know. Lots of regards to yourself and Cie.[28]

Besides sending Norris a copy of *Flappers and Philosophers*
(1920), Fitzgerald had urged the reprinting of all the books of
Frank Norris. He was serious enough to pursue the matter with
H. L. Mencken, who at that time was publishing some of
Fitzgerald's own writings in *The Smart Set*. Mencken's response
was direct and enthusiastic:

The Norris scheme is excellent and it goes without saying that I'll
be glad to help it along. The impediment is the fact that most of the
Norris books, if not all, are owned by Doubleday, Page & Co., a very
lousy bunch. However, Charles Norris might be able to get control of

them. A Man's Woman is bad stuff,[29] but it ought to go in the series. A good man to do the Blix preface would be George Sterling.[30] He took me on a nighthack jaunt around San Francisco to visit its scenes. You ought to do one yourself.[31]

Although Fitzgerald did not submit such a preface, Mencken himself wrote a glowing one for *Vandover and the Brute*.

Nevertheless, even as early as 1920 Fitzgerald shared with Charles Norris a generosity in his dealings with fellow writers. He no doubt discussed the Frank Norris edition with Mencken in some detail. Charles Norris clearly thought enough of Fitzgerald's idea to enlist the help of Doubleday, Mencken, and other friends and see the project through to its successful completion in 1928.

Norris's name continued to crop up in Fitzgerald's writings as well as in his scrapbooks. In a 1920 letter to his literary agent, Harold Ober, Fitzgerald placed Norris in the company of James Branch Cabell and Theodore Dreiser: "Do you think a story like C. G. Norris' *Salt* or Cabell's *Jurgen* or Dreiser's *Jenny Gerhard* [sic] would have one chance in a million to be sold serially?"[32] In a letter to his editor, Maxwell Perkins, dated 3 February [1920?], Fitzgerald praised Frank Norris highly and added: "I told you last November that I'd read *Salt* by his brother Charles and was quite enthusiastic about it." On 1 October 1921 Fitzgerald mentioned Charles Norris again to Maxwell Perkins: "I have not seen one single review for 2 months but here are my prognostications for the fall. I have only read the 1*st* of these books. (1.) Brass by Charles Norris.— Worthy, honest, thorough but fundamentally undistinguished."[33] That Fitzgerald's enthusiasm for Charles Norris's *Salt* was still burning brightly some three years later is dramatically evident in his 1924 letter to Maxwell Perkins rating Leslie Wagstaff with George Hurstwood and Tom Buchanan. One year later the creator of the brother in *Salt* shared his own views on Dreiser's creation. In December 1925 Charles Norris declared that if he "were to pick out the character who for twenty years . . . has stirred me, and wrung my heart with sympathy and pity, I must submit Hurstwood in Dreiser's 'Sister Carrie.' Hurstwood, because there is no truer portrait— man or woman—in any book I've ever read. . . . Hurstwood, because his moral degradation, his slow crumbling, and the disintegration of his soul, spirit and body as the direct result of his crime is masterly conceived, masterly presented, and masterly worked out."[34]

As late as February 1936, in his brilliant essay "The Crack Up," Fitzgerald was still presumably hearing that "booming repetition of [Charles Norris's] title phrase [strategically placed] at the beginning of each section" [of *Salt*], for he uses the precise biblical (New Testament) phrase to end his own ("profoundly felt") essay: "Ye are the salt of the earth. But if the salt hath lost its savour, wherewith shall it be salted?" Matthew 5:13.

Although the evidence for direct literary influence is inconclusive, it is sufficient to suggest that echoes from Norris's fiction not only remained in Fitzgerald's mind, but found their way into his writings. There are some echoes of *Brass* in *Gatsby*, but parallels between details in *Salt* and descriptions in Fitzgerald's early writings are even stronger. Compare, for instance, the following passages from *Salt* and "May Day" (a story Fitzgerald probably wrote not long after his excited reading of Charles Norris's second novel). In an early chapter of *Salt*, detailing Griffith Adams's prep school and college days with an impressionistic vividness, Norris sensuously describes Griffith's dream girl, Margaret Sothern, the belle of the Delta Om's fraternity dance: "He was able to recall the scene afterward . . . their gay chatter . . . his own black back and bent head, the long tapering white arms and the shining hair of the exquisite figure . . . the perfume of crushed flowers, sachet and the fine scent of cigarettes pervaded the air, and from without came . . . faint laughter . . ." (93). In "May Day" Fitzgerald similarly describes a fraternity dance, capturing in a Renoir-like manner the first appearance of Gordon Sterett's former sweetheart, Edith Bradin:

She . . . stood looking over the shoulders of a black dress in front of her at the groups of Yale men who flitted like dignified black moths. . . . the heavy fragrance left by the passage to and fro of many scented young beauties—rich perfumes and the fragile memory-laden dust of fragrant powders. This odor drifting out acquired the tang of cigarette smoke in the hall and then settled sensuously down the stairs and permeated the ballroom where the Gamma Psi dance was to be held. . . .

She thought of her own appearance. Her bare arms . . . were powdered to a creamy white. She knew they looked very soft and white and would gleam like milk against the black backs that were to silhouette them tonight. The hairdressing had been a success; her reddish mass of hair was . . . an arrogant marvel of mobile curves. She was a complete, infinitely delicate, quite perfect thing of beauty, flowing in an even line from a complex coiffure to two small slim feet.[35]

The silhouetting black backs, the gleaming, bare white arms and shining reddish hair, the exquisite, quite perfect figure, the perfume mingling with cigarette smoke "pervading" or "permeating" the atmosphere form the impressionistic core of both descriptions. Fitzgerald has transformed Norris's descriptions through his more precise diction and subtle poetic rhythms. For, like Dreiser, one of his heroes, Norris excels in *Salt* less with felicity of expression than careful piling up of well-observed details that provide solid and believable backdrops for his real characters. The result of his careful selection and imaginative arrangement is painstakingly crafted material that Fitzgerald could spin into his own filigrees of golden prose. When Fitzgerald wasn't joining the chorus of critics who lavished overt praise on Norris's strengths, he was paying him the higher compliment of imitation, albeit with variation.

In *Salt* there is, predictably, evidence of Norris's own sources in the many echoes from both his life and the books he himself had admired. Like his maternal grandmother, Maybelle was born in Taunton, Massachusetts. For Griffith's life in Cambridge Norris drew from his own observations during the year he and Gertrude lived there while Frank was studying at Harvard. Griffith's sexual initiation when "he was half drunk," leaving him in "utter disgust" (72), and the sobering result of his "first brutal awareness of sex" (17–19) are almost identical to Vandover's experiences. The results of venereal disease contracted by Griffith's fraternity brothers parallel the deadly encounter of Vandover's Dolly Haight (and look forward to a similar experience in Norris's *Bricks without Straw*). Griffith terminates his sexual relationship with a coed for fear of VD rather than for moral reasons. Like a typical Frank Norris heroine, Rissie Rumsey displays "even little rows of teeth like kernels on an ear of corn." And Mr. Rumsey in his rocking chair, unable to find work, is straight out of Dreiser's description of Hurstwood. Charles is at his best, however, when he is not imitating literature but transmuting life.

Assessment

Norris's greater ability to turn personal experiences into fiction is part of what makes *Salt* a much better novel than *The Amateur.* Drawing heavily from his own experiences at private schools and Berkeley, he gives a convincing, if one-sided, picture of Eastern private schools and Midwestern universities before World War I. Griffith's perverse pride at having endured sadistic fraternity hazing, for example, is set against Norris's graphic description of the ritual and its results:

> Wearily he sought his room, eager for his bed. When he came to undress he found that his underclothes were stuck in places to his bruised legs. With a quick jerk he freed them too tired to save himself the extra twinge of pain. But he was aghast at the sight of his purple, misshapen thighs, the fore and hind parts of his legs above the knee. Great welts swollen to the size of heavy ropes criss-crossed one another like the woven strands in a doormat. . . . there were abrasions like the broken surface of decaying fruit, the raw meat protruding through the rents. A flow of blood started by the quick rending of his underclothes from these ugly bruises, trickled in thin wiggling streams between the fine hairs upon his legs. (86)

Norris is more effective, if less grim, in his detailed descriptions of fraudulent practices in advertising and big business. He also creates a richer, more fully developed main character in *Salt,* human in both his contradictions and consistencies. Foreshadowing the self-deceptive inconsistencies of Fitzgerald's Nick Carraway, Norris notes those times when "Griffith believes he had an unusually strong character" (57). By following Kynnersley's Emersonian advice to take the risks of the solitary performer, Griffith gains the maturity to live a more moral life and rekindle the early love of his second nurse, reinforced by the loyalty of his brother and the sustained warmth and goodness of the Pohli family.

The strongest and freshest aspects of the novel, however,

remain Norris's Rissie and Leslie. They both approach Dickensian genius. In spite of the "sallow unhealthy skin which she attempted to conceal with much powder" and the "strong pungent perfume of musk" with which she drenched herself, despite her "simper[ing] a great deal, throwing languorous, flirtatious glances under lowered lids . . . ," she appeals to Griffith. She is a wonderful dancer; he enjoys the kisses from her full lips covered with carmen paste that "reminded him of the camphor ice his mother had rubbed upon his chapped lips as a boy," and he "literally hungered for her caresses" (161, 255). It is her caresses that seduce him into marriage after Griffith's boss has humiliated and fired him. There are light moments in the marriage, as when "Griffith squirted a siphon bottle through the keyhole . . . drenching her beribboned night-gown," prompting their "shrieks of laughter," but more often than not her faults are offensive to him (260).

He would come tired from work to a filthy apartment: "Lines of brown sediment along the sides of the tub marked the height of various soapy baths, and nests of dust and dirt collected in cracks and corners. Waterbugs thrived everywhere. On the vent in the kitchen sink there was invariably a little collection of refuse,—seeds, wet crusts, tea leaves, burnt matches, ends of string, kernels of stewed corn and chips of egg shells. Griffith protested; Clarisse met his objections with the indifferent assertion she could not bear to touch the mess" (271). He is too ashamed of her to accept an invitation to the McCleish wedding reception: "He knew she would simper when she met Margaret, and look reproachfully at Archie as she held out her hand stiffly to him, asking him dramatically why he had not been to see them. She would gaze about the assemblage under affectedly lowered lids, step mincingly from room to room, pick with elaborate daintiness at whatever refreshments were served, assuming a languid, bored expression, hopelessly transparent. He could not permit her to make herself ridiculous before his old friends" (290).

Despite her prominent faults, Griffith is patient and tender with her, particularly during her difficult pregnancy. He is deeply moved by her sudden death some days after the birth of their only child: "An emotional paralysis descended upon Griffith after the first moments of grief" (319). Weeks later, at the sight of her "gay little crepe wrapper" in the abandoned apartment, he realizes that he "missed her terribly; he forgot her complaints and her artificiality; he remembered her caresses, her tenderness and love" (327).

Whether or not he is, with Hurstwood and Tom Buchanan, among "the three best characters in American fiction" between 1904 and 1924, Leslie Wagstaff is decidedly a Dickensian triumph. When not working as the general passenger agent for the railroad or sleeping in his overcrowded apartment, Leslie reads the newspaper and drinks with steady determination. A widower, he takes all of his meals in restaurants that serve liquor. "He was a solitary, morose, silent little man whom nobody loved and who, outside of Griffith, loved nobody" (153). Using the brush strokes of a meticulous artist, Charles outlines this quiet man who places "a soft small hand" on his brother's shoulder; then he repeats details of Leslie's appearance, dress and action, blending them consummately. As Fitzgerald insists in "The Rich Boy," he begins with an individual and creates a type: "A little man with a pale expressionless face. . . . He wore an unkempt Van Dyke beard, and the mustache covering his upper lip hung long and ragged over his mouth. The hair upon his face and upon the top of his head where it had begun to thin was darkly red. His eyes were sunken and sombre, with no light in them. Griffith was struck with his unhealthy paleness. The face above the thick, untidy beard was colorless as white paper" (128). Although Leslie "often got on his nerves" and Griffith "had a contempt for his baggy, ill-fitting clothes," Griffith discovers in him a firm core of affection and loyalty: "In a moment of profound depression following a call at his office of a collector . . . of his college bills . . . he had turned to his brother and asked him for a loan. . . . The next day Leslie had brought home a cheque and handed it to him without a word . . . (152). Regarding Leslie's personal habits:

It was whiskey, whiskey, whiskey from early morning until the last thing before he went to bed. He ate practically nothing. Often he went silently out to dinner with Griffith and watched him eat a hearty meal, while he sat smoking one cigarette after another, slowly drinking two, three,—sometimes four ponies of his favorite liquor. A definite aroma of tobacco and alcohol pervaded him. He did not bathe with the regularity of most men; he took a bath not oftener than once a month, and the odor that enveloped him grew more noticeable as the interval lengthened. During the day at his office he helped himself continually from a bottle he kept in his lower desk drawer. At nine o'clock in the evening, sometimes at eight he went quietly to bed, taking the newspaper with him, read half-an-hour to an hour before getting himself his final drink and extinguishing his light.

. . . A printed sheet of morning or evening daily was constantly before his eyes; he read line by line, carefully turning the big pages, doubling them neatly back upon themselves, creasing the fold, smoothing the sheet so it would not wrinkle. He spent hours over the various news items; he never failed to read the stock market reports, the death column, the weather predictions, and frequently the want ads from first to last. These were of equal interest to him as the news that was double headlined on the first page. He never referred to what he read. The daily papers provided him with his only amusement; he read their columns to occupy his mind. The routine of office work, whiskey, and newspaper reading, were the three elements which made up his existence. (152–53)

While Griffith is a struggling apprentice in the wool business, Leslie sends money with the letters he writes to him "every two or three weeks. . . . Griffith had come to love his brother" when "he received a letter informing him of Leslie's paralytic stroke. . . . Griffith found Leslie in a private sanitarium . . . in a little whitewalled room. . . . his frowsy head . . . looked so small among the pillows! On the chair beside his bed was a crumpled newspaper and a tumbler with a swallow of whiskey at its bottom" (347). Griffith tries to comfort him but "Leslie was resigned to his fate. He had no complaints to make. He hoped only that he would not live too long; it was so difficult to manage his paper with one hand that he grew too tired to read, and the doctor only allowed him twelve ounces of whiskey a day" (348). Two months later he is dead.

With growing strength of character Griffith refuses to contest his brother's old will, refusing to accept money that "was not of his [own] earning" (349). And the reader is convinced of Leslie's positive influence as it transcends youthful dislike and adult denunciation. Despite his alcohol-besotted, uneventful life, Leslie's steady undercurrent of love and loyalty reinforces the more admirable aspects of Griffith's character, the qualities that had earlier won the support of Miss Fisher and Mr. Kynnersly.

The novel itself remains one of Charles Norris's best. Contrary to the *Springfield Republican* claim that the title is irrelevant to the story, he has written a novel in the firm tradition of books dealing with the education of a young man, including Samuel Butler's *The Way Of All Flesh* and Henry Adams's classic *Education*. Like those of Butler and Adams, Norris's portrayal drew attack from the Establishment. Charles N. Eliot of Harvard wrote to him (29 July 1918) regarding his "theory" in *Salt* "about the evils, in boarding schools and colleges." Eliot defends prep schools and Harvard and supposes that "in portraying the weak, unprincipled, sensual and foolish Griffith [Norris] meant to indicate to boys and young men that they had better not be like him. . . . but if I were a writer of novels, I think I should have more confidence in the usefulness of portraying positively strong and noble characters than feeble and ignoble ones."[36] Norris anticipated such an attack in the concluding sentence of his author's note: "The book represents a painstaking effort to transcribe the results of personal observations over a number of years, and to make the principal character of the tale a type of American youth which is, I believe, to all unfortunately familiar."

He has done so, admirably.

Chapter Three
Brass and *Bread*

Brass: Plot

The time period of *Brass, A Novel of Marriage* ranges from 1852 through the Spanish American War in 1898 and the San Francisco earthquake in 1906 to shortly before World War I. Norris's main focus is on less than twenty years of Philip Baldwin's existence, a record of the fluctuations of his love life and business affairs from his first infatuation as a twenty-two-year-old ranch foreman until, as a middle-aged San Francisco insurance broker, he endures a marriage with a woman he has grown to hate.

Philip is the son of Judge Samuel Baldwin, an ex-prospector, gambler, expert in law, who is a generous and courteous, if unfaithful, husband to the patient, religious, indefatigable Matilda who inherited the ranch her husband and son run. Philip falls in love with Marjorie Jones, a hired fruit picker, the day after he has first kissed Rosemary Church, his childhood sweetheart. Shortly after Philip's and Marjorie's marriage, his only brother Harry weds Rosemary, and before long seventeen-year-old Lucy Baldwin marries Philip's enterprising new partner, Wilbur Lansing.

Despite the help of Marjorie's older sister Constance, Philip's and Marjorie's passionate love survives neither mother-in-law interference nor their own bickering over money and lodging and Marjorie's choice of flighty theatrical friends. The Jones's housekeeper, Mrs. Grotenberg, feeds Philip's discontent with sympathy for him and denigration of Marjorie's wifely neglect. Marjorie leaves their small son with Constance and runs off to New York with Ray North, a married artist.

Two years later Philip falls in love with the beautiful, cultured Mary Rowland, who returns his love but leaves him when her Roman Catholic sensibility is shocked by the knowledge of his divorce. Stunned, almost suicidal, Philip allows Mrs. Grotenberg to salve his wounds. The period she lives with him in a cottage in the Berkeley hills is the happiest extended time of his life; but this relationship too is terminated when, knowing she is dying of cancer, Mrs. Grotenberg commits suicide rather than burden him. Lonely once more, Philip reluctantly gives in to the urgings of his sister Lucy and her society friends and marries the vain Leila Veil.

Although he and his brother-in-law have both made much money in insurance, real estate, and speculation, their financial stability rests mainly on Wilbur's ingenuity. When, frustrated by Lucy's sexual coldness, Wilbur runs away with Flossie, another married woman, Philip's bankruptcy follows quickly. Leila grows colder as they are forced to move to more frugal quarters. For a time their child, Lucy II, is all that holds them together. The insurance business that sister Lucy's new million-aire husband sends Philip restores only the Baldwins' material well-being. His business is sound. The marriage is dead. At the novel's end Leila has a separate bedroom and separate friends. Philip's only consolations are the affection of daughter Lucy and the solitary pleasures of the *table d'hote* at a downtown restaurant.

Reception

There is far more information in the Norris family papers on Charles's third novel than on any of the others. He and Kathleen kept one of their scrapbooks virtually filled with newspaper and magazine clippings charting the notoriety of both *Brass* and its author throughout America and England. As the book of a writer who, because of his own reputation and the popularity of Kathleen, had become better known, it also received a fuller press than did either *The Amateur* or *Salt*. Both Charles and Kathleen granted interviews excerpted by newspapers across the country. Almost overnight, in the eyes of their public, they became marriage experts. One interview granted to the *New York Times Book Review* on 12 March 1922, entitled "The Norrises Discuss Marriage," offers helpful insights into the novel it helped to advertise.

The article recounts how "Years ago he had read H. G. Wells's novel, *Marriage,* as a magazine [the *American*] editor and . . . cut 60,000 words out of it in order to serialize the story. *Marriage* treated a single couple . . . the book was not typical of married life. It carried through the life of an exceptional pair. Therefore, Mr. Norris explained, in doing his book he had to sacrifice construction and drag in a dozen couples and plot enough for a dozen novels." Claiming to have written *Brass* "four times before he was satisfied with it," he admitted that "there are about three times as many unhappy marriages in *Brass* than there are happy ones" but that, despite the unfair proportion, "he needed such a number to give a fair exposition of his thesis which was not the happy marriage but the reasons for the unhappy ones." Regarding marriage in the United States, he is more outspoken: "There are so many unfortunate marriages. . . . And chief among them [is] the one where there is disgusting incivility . . . between husband and wife. I think occasionally infidelity is less heinous than rudeness. The spectacle of a man shouting at his wife, 'Shutup!' for instance, is enough to make me believe in divorce."[1] In another interview, in the *Los Angeles Express* on 27 October 1921, he is more explicit: "If, for example, a rude inconsiderate man could be told by his wife: 'If you again fail to bathe properly, if you cough in my face or neglect or insult me I will leave you tomorrow morning'—and if he knew she could do it— . . . there would be more courtesy in marriage and less divorce. As to children—we accept death. Why not divorce?"[2]

For the *New York Times* account Charles admitted that when he "started to explore the question of married life" he "was against divorce for any reason." Pressed for measures to reverse the increasing divorce rate in America, Charles "threw caution to the winds":

We ought to have a national marriage law . . . that shall define the ages which couples must be to get married: that shall make imperative a physical examination and see that the couple are eugenically fitted to mate: that shall provide that the husband is in fit circumstances to support a family. . . . People who intend to get married should be investigated. . . . It should be discovered whether the man has been married before and why the first marriage holds no longer. It should be made plain whether the woman has any entangling alliances.

How much the accelerated publicity campaign helped the considerable sales of *Brass* is difficult to judge, but it is clear that

Norris's outspoken declarations regarding divorce tainted its critical reception, particularly with the more conservative periodicals. Controversial subject matter together with certain stylistic and structural weaknesses prompted the novel's decidedly mixed reviews.

Edwin Francis Edgett, writing for the *Boston Evening Transcript,* on 24 August 1921, jumped on Norris's claim that for the sake of his thesis he had "had to sacrifice construction and drag in . . . couples and plot enough for a dozen novels." Edgett saw *Brass*'s "pages crowded with incidents and personalities and although they are brought together in coherent form, there are so many and so varied, his point of view changes so frequently and so suddenly, that the story creates the effect of a panorama rather than carries the feeling of a carefully composed and well ordered picture." He did praise Norris's "vivid word paintings of the city and its people" and allowed that although he is "repetitious in the extreme" it is "always with an apparent purpose."[3] Although she acknowledged that Norris had written "a careful, conscientious and realistic study" in *Brass,* Louise Maunsell Field liked it even less. Writing for the *New York Times Book Review,* on 25 September 1921, she complained that "The book is not well written" and that "economy of words seems to be . . . unknown to the author."[4] The reviewer for *Literary Digest,* on 29 October 1921, was somewhat kinder: "Tho the novel is badly in need of cutting, there is much in it that is very good, the best being the description of Philip's first marriage. From the moment he and Marjorie are married in the cheap little flat until the time of their final separation, the portrayal is . . . convincing enough in and by itself to make *Brass* a notable novel."[5] The *Dial* in "Briefer Mention," November 1921, made clear its preference by pillorying two writers in one sentence: "Neither adorning his platitude with any visible ecstacy of manner, nor pointing his tale with sharp and illuminating gestures, the author of *Salt* tells this second story with the gravid exuberance of Dreiser."[6] The *American Hebrew,* on 2 December 1921, saw the literary parallel in more positive light: "Out of the west a new Dreiser has come. . . . One cannot put [*Brass*] down, and one leaves the last page with real regret. . . . But realistic as it is *Brass* is absolutely without humor. The book does very well without it—but its

absence offers an excellent explanation of the reason why all
these marriages fail—for none can succeed without the saving
grace of a sense of humor."[7] Samuel Abbott of the *New York
Tribune,* on 25 September 1921, felt that *Brass* "lacks heart
and . . . is effeminate in spirit where it demands the harsh
surgery of a masculine hand. Were it . . . stripped of its precise
prose picturing pins and buttons, and just permitted to get to its
goals quickly and decisively, it would be a much finer and
greater story."[8] The *Minneapolis Journal* for 30 August 1921
took the novel less seriously: "The hero of *Brass* is said to be
maddened by the perpetual coldness of his wife's [Leila's] feet.
Why did he not get the poor thing a soapstone and so retain his
good nature?"[9] Objecting piously to Philip's time of "peace or
contentment" with his mistress, the *Lexington* (Kentucky) *Herald,* on 18 September 1921, called *Brass* "an odious picture
of odious contradictions, at times rather odiously well
written. . . ."[10] Any doubt that Mrs. Grundy still lived in 1921
was also put to rest by the *New York Independent:* "The reader of
American novels is between the devil and the deep sea. If he
care not at all for the inane school of Pollyanna, he has no other
choice than . . . the grim, grubby crowd of writers who produce 'Dirt' and 'Clay' and 'Gloom.' . . . I have yet to read a
Pollyanna novel. . . . But after two years of American 'modern-
ists' and 'realists,' I am led to believe that the cesspool school of
novelists is as false to life and art as Pollyanna in her most
maddening phases. . . . Mr. Norris's 'Brass' drags in its intermi-
nable coils forever and forever."[11] The *St. Paul News,* in
October 1921, defended Norris's presentation of "his thesis
without offering any solution for the matter. . . . Snaggle-
toothed old women, frustrated in everything save an outlet for
their gossip, can prove to you in 10 or 15 minutes that marriage
as a celestial state is impossible."[12] The *New York Tribune* in a
second review, on 16 October 1921, saw "a frank treatment of
affairs of sex and divorce, with little or no trace of vulgarity. A
novel that wins one's respect the more he thinks of it after
leaving the final pages. One of the very few [American] novels
of worth of 1921. . . ."[13]

Of the negative reviews F. Scott Fitzgerald's "Poor Old
Marriage" in the *Bookman,* November 1921, was perhaps the
most telling. He acknowledged that "some of the scenes are

excellent—Philip's first courtship, his reunion with Marjorie after their first separation, his final meeting with her . . ." but his overall review was grudgingly but decidedly unfavorable: "In the glow of [*Salt*] I read *Brass* and suffered a distinct disappointment. . . . It is a cold book throughout. . . ." He saw none of the "fine delicacy" found in Frank Norris's work. "*Brass* . . . becomes at times merely the shocker—the harrowing description of Leila's feet could only be redeemed by a little humor, of which none is forthcoming. Early in the book one finds the following sentence: 'He inflated his chest . . . pounding with shut fists the hard surface of his breast, alternating digging his fingertips into the firm flesh about his nipples.' Here he has missed his mark entirely. I gather from the context that he has intended to express the tremendous vitality of his hero in the early morning. Not questioning the accuracy of the details in themselves it is none the less obvious that he has chosen entirely the *wrong* details. He has given us a glimpse not into Philip's virility but into the Bronx zoo." Fitzgerald concludes that *Brass* is neither "entirely new and fresh and profoundly felt" nor "a tour de force by a man of exceptional talent."[14]

Despite the reservations voiced by Fitzgerald and half the reviewers, *Brass* continued to sell. The *Dayton* (Ohio) *News* announced on Christmas that *Brass* was "in its twenty-fourth edition and the demand for it is constantly growing."[15] Earlier that fall Dutton had collected key quotations from favorable reviews by Zona Gale, Rupert Hughes, Arthur T. Vance, Fannie Hurst, William Irwin, and FPA (of the *New York Tribune*) for an advertisement which appeared in such places as the *New York Times Book Review and Magazine* section on 6 October 1921.[16] Zona Gale, whose review for the *New York Evening Post,* on 17 September 1921, Dutton also printed in its entirety, called the novel "magnificent . . . whether or not his thesis is convincing . . . an honest work conceived and carried off . . . with superb disdain for tricky effect and with a fidelity to its characters which is not so much the artist creating as the scientific spirit observing. . . . On the whole a brilliant novel . . . whose validity lies where it ought to be—in the unconscious."[17] In letters to Norris, E. Phillips Oppenheim, on 5 October 1923, called *Brass* "a wonderful study of the most discussed of our social institutions," and Sinclair Lewis, after a lecture on the novel's "needless colloquialisms," wrote that *Brass* "indicates that there is no reason why [Norris] should not go to the very *top* of the heap of writers—writers, anywhere, in any country."[18] Fannie Hurst saw fit to write two letters in praise of *Brass.* To editor John Macrae: "I think it rides Norris into the rank of foremost American novelists, not on any of the artificially stimulated ripples created by the art-for-God-sakes, rocking the boat, but on the booming wave of truth." To Norris: "I think *Brass* belongs to the upper ten of native novels. . . ."[19]

With help from these famous writers and a supportive review from H. L. Mencken, *Brass* remained on the best-seller lists for many months, vying for sales with Fitzgerald's *The Beautiful and Damned* and, along with H. G. Wells's *Outline of History* and G. B. Shaw's *Back to Methuselah,* one of the six books most in demand at the Chicago Public Library. Mencken objected to the debates that "are usually dull. . . . But in presenting his facts as opposed to his theories . . . , Norris shows all of the skill that revealed itself in *Salt.* Nothing escapes him. He paints the everyday American with truly horrible fidelity, missing not a single wart, or post-prandial belch, or red spot where the collar rubs. His people live and move—clerks, social pushers, good businessmen, farmers, neighborhood Bryans, drab wives, chianti Bohemians. Even the children of the tale are alive—an almost unbelievable feat. . . ."[20]

On 13 April 1922 the *Chicago Examiner* printed the following news item: "Warner Brothers are conducting a beauty contest which will give four embryonic film aspirants an opportunity to appear in their four pictures, 'From Rags to Riches,' 'Little Heroes of the Street,' 'Brass,' and 'Main Street.' Here's your chance!"[21] Less than two months later, on 3 June 1922, the *Montreal Star* announced: "Charles G. Norris, the brilliant California novelist, whose latest work 'Brass' is being picturized, has voiced the opinion that too many minds spoil an author's brainchild when transformed to the screen. And never was a truer word said."[22] The "picturized" version of *Brass* was not a success; but publicity surrounding it kept the spotlight on Norris's novel. Fitzgerald pasted in one of his scrapbooks (which include over twenty clippings mentioning his own name and books with those of either Kathleen, Charles Norris, or both when their novels are listed in the top six or ten books sold in bookstores or circulated in libraries) a clipping headed "Read 'Em and Weep" which contains the following account:

> The latest movie manufacturers are the Warner brothers. They produce stories without reading them. Their art is legerdemain. For instance, they could put 'Macbeth' in a hat and bring out 'Peter Rabbit.' They did the stunt with Norris' 'Brass'—and it came out Warner Brothers' brass. They are hypnotists, too. . . . F. Scott Fitzgerald stepped forward with 'The Beautiful and Damned.' They made a few passes at him and when he opened his eyes and looked at his story he thought he was Louisa M. Alcott. . . . We hear that 'Main Street' will soon come forth with marked civic improvements.[23]

The Forging

Brass's popularity with the reading public (by February 1922 it was in its fortieth printing) was in proportion to the energy Charles put into its creation; again he had drawn heavily on his own experiences. The biographical influences are as numerous as in his first two novels. In describing Wilbur Lansing's profitable business deals,[24] Charles drew on his own successful financial ventures. Philip's second love, Mary Rowland, a large woman, reads Browning to him in the same eloquently dramatic manner as Gertrude Doggett Norris. For the discussion of desertion and divorce Charles needed to go no further than his parents' unsuccessful marriage. Just as vivid are the parallels between the Norrises' first idyllic summer at La Estancia and the ecstatic account of Philip's visit to Harry's and Rosemary's ranch. Details of his stay come straight out of Charles's memories, down to the specific games played and the barbecued meat cooked and eaten amid their redwood groves (414–15).

Echoes from Dreiser also continue, including a reminder of Drouet's gift of two crisp new twenty-dollar greenbacks to Carrie: "[Philip] found three twenties, dropped them into [Mrs. Grotenberg's] purse and tossed it back into her lap" (277). *Brass* also shows traces of Charles's debt to Frank. The description of "Judge" Baldwin's physiognomy and deeds are

strikingly similar to those of "the Governor," Magnus Derek, in
The Octopus. Sharing Derek's gold fever, Baldwin had "pros-
pected, gambled, and gallivanted. He made money over night
and lost it in the morning." Like Derek, "in all affairs of the
heart he played the part of a gentleman" (9). Philip's temper
and actions are very like Annixter's when he, like Annixter, is
frustrated in love and strikes out irrationally at a hired hand.
His youthful show of physical strength to impress Marjorie is
very like McTeague's attempts to impress Trina: "[Phil] amused
himself by lifting heavy chairs by the leg with one hand or
'chinning' himself, clinging by finger-tips to the frame at the top
of the bathroom door. . . . with her small fingers [Marjorie]
would try to make an impression on his hard contracted
biceps . . . and she would thump at his bare chest with her
small fists and laugh at her ridiculous efforts" (80–81). Charles's
many descriptions of interior decorations in questionable taste
are as effective as many of Frank's in *McTeague* and *The Octopus,*
and similar to them. Philip's office, for instance, is indelibly
preserved:

> Above the three decks in a redwood frame, the rough ragged bark
> still adhering, hung a large panoramic view of "Carlsbad-by-the-Sea."
> . . . There were other photographs: automobile picnic parties in a
> redwood grove, a new railroad station, mission style, the name
> conspicuous in large gilt letters, a gondola bedecked with roses,
> gliding through pond lilies. . . .
> On the opposite side of the office . . . more photographs adorned
> [the] wall: a man parting gigantic corn stalks, two laughing children
> peering from a heap of oranges, a row of cows standing knee-deep in a
> willow-shaded stream. On a large square table in the middle of the
> office were arranged neat stacks of colored folders and circulars, and
> between these were small piles of corn-ears, sample bags of beans
> and dry alfalfa, enormous walnuts, a pyramid of dried prunes, and
> ornamental glass jars containing large preserved pears and peaches.
> (163–64)

The photographs recall aspects of the art festival at the San
Francisco fair in *The Octopus:* "In the foreground, and to the left,
under the shade of a live-oak, stood a couple of reddish cows,
knee-deep in a patch of yellow poppies, while in the right-hand
corner, to balance the composition, was placed a girl in a pink

and white sunbonnet, in which the shadows were indicated by broad dashes of blue paint."[25] But perhaps the most dramatically interesting parallels are in the San Francisco wedding ceremonies of the Baldwins and the McTeagues. Charles recounts: "The words of the service began but Philip was distracted. Cablecars droned heavily by outside, clanging their bells, a delivery wagon rattled past on the cobbled pavement, factory whistles announced the noon hour in strident keys, the grinding whir of the coffee mill in the grocery below could be plainly distinguished. Gradually he became conscious of the clergyman's words . . ." (77). Compare this with *McTeague*'s "Outside the noise of the street rose to the windows in muffled undertones, a cable car rumbled past, a newsboy went by chanting the evening papers; from somewhere in the building itself came a persistent noise of sawing."[26]

There is evidence in *Brass* that Charles continued to influence Fitzgerald, particularly in *The Great Gatsby*. The influence may well have carried into the 1930s. In *Brass* a despondent Philip, abandoned by Mary Rowland, imagines his name in headlines: "He looked down at the lapping slate-colored water . . . and let his mind play with the thought of a hasty jump, the cold submersion, the cry of alarm. . . . He saw the newspaper headings in the morning: 'Business-man Commits Suicide—Philip Baldwin of Baldwin and Lansing Drowns—Unhappy Love Affair Asserted by Friends to Have Been Cause of Rash Act" (206). Near the end of Fitzgerald's 1931 essay "My Lost City":

All is lost save memory, yet sometimes I imagine myself reading, with curious interest, a *Daily News* of the issue of 1945:

> MAN OF FIFTY RUNS AMUCK IN NEW YORK
> Fitzgerald Feathered Many Love Nests Cutie Avers
> Bumped Off by Outraged Gunman[27]

Results

But any final judgments on the merits of *Brass* rest neither on Norris's sources nor on those authors he influenced but on the novel itself. There are, admittedly, stylistic flaws in *Brass*.

There are too many clichés, too much awkward phraseology, and too many words. Sinclair Lewis, who was "delighted by *Brass*," calling it "strong, resolute, solid, true," justly chided Charles for what is one of the novel's major weaknesses:

> You must be more severe with your style. Occasionally you use quite needless colloquialisms . . . in straight narration and description. . . . In one place you said that a woman's frock was "cunning" . . . —a feeble misuse of the word—and in another place you spoke of something as being "all fussed up" or "fixed up". . . . These, for a writer of your discrimination, are inexcusable; are certainly not to be excused by any raging insistence that you care more for content than for style; for the one thing that style does do is to elucidate the content. I wonder how sternly and meticulously you revise? You ought to, for you have in you the very biggest things.[28]

Mencken was also right when he objected to the debates as "usually dull and often quite banal," but his praise of the fine descriptions in *Brass* has an even greater validity. Both Mencken and Fitzgerald point to another strength, Norris's success in drawing characters who live rather than "remain bloodless, lifeless ciphers." The variety of characters praised is alone a tribute to his success at characterization. Fitzgerald called Marjorie and Philip's mother "the best characters in the book."[29] Mencken's admiration went to Mrs. Grotenberg, whose episode is "strongest," with "the utmost reality and . . . a touch of genuine poetry." Fannie Hurst wrote, "I hate *most* of your characters. I believe them! . . . [Mrs. Grotenberg is] one of the strongest portrayals . . . that I've encountered in fiction."[30]

Although *Brass* is in need of cutting, many of the scenes are as finely chiseled as the carefully defined characters. Fitzgerald aptly praised Norris's "excellent" scenes involving Philip's and Marjorie's courtship, reunion, and final meeting. The description of his first marriage is also excellent, as Norris captures at once the joys of youthful love and the irony of Philip's incipient dissatisfaction with the object of his love. His son Paul's resemblance to the meddling grandmother is a constant irritation to Philip. Norris notes this at the moment of the baby's birth: "He was interested and curious about the baby; but the fact that he was now a father touched his vanity. . . . But when the nurse brought home the child his enthusiasm was somewhat chilled. The little face was a weazened comic replica of Marjorie's mother; the child had the same close-set eyes, the same elongated, knobular nose; he was all Jones. The only baby Philip had ever known had been his sister, Lucy, and he had imagined in a dim sort of way that all babies were fat and jolly with blue eyes and flaxen hair" (120–21). Toward the end of the novel, Philip and Paul (now a sullen teenager) watch Marjorie (now a film actress) on the screen of a Nickelodeon in a role that ironically contrasts with her desertion of her own baby years before: "at the end of the picture Marjorie was shown in a 'close-up,' bending with streaming eyes over her little one, and straining the baby to her breast. The words she was supposed to utter . . . were flashed upon the screen: 'My baby!—My little one! You shall never leave your mother's arms again. Death—and death alone, shall separate us!'" (401).

Peter Clark MacFarland wrote perceptively, on 14 May 1922, to Kathleen about Charles's eye for detail in his descriptions in *Brass* of the California landscape: "I have always been awed by the 'atmosphere' of *The Octopus,* and methinks I saw this brotherly kinship of Charles G. flash out in the quivering sunshine of the Vaca Valley. . . ."[31] The realism does more than occasionally rise "to the genuinely tragic; sometimes reminding one . . . of the unrelenting qualities of *McTeague.*"[32]

Brass is a readable book, thoughtfully considered and, for the most part, well executed. It holds its own with most of the other books that shared the best-seller spotlight in 1921–22, including W. Somerset Maugham's *The Trembling of a Leaf* and Sherwood Anderson's *The Triumph of Egg.* It stands well beside novels the *New York Evening Globe,* on 21 October 1921, lumped with it under "Recent fiction we have not liked," which included Ben Hecht's *Erik Dorn* and John Dos Passos's *Three Soldiers.*[33] The *Detroit News* of 9 October 1921, reviewing *Brass* beside Kathleen's latest novel, made a valid comparison. After light pleasantries about *Beloved Women,* it stressed that "*Brass* is something else. Mrs. Norris . . . has written on the fripperies and vanities of life. But *Brass* is life itself. . . . There is no tremendously big situation, no heroics, in the whole 452 pages of rather finely printed type. But it is all life, hard, cruel, tragic even, but life nevertheless."³⁴

Perhaps what William Curtis said about *Brass* in 1921 is even more appropriate now: "[It is] solidly constructed, bearing evidence of a great deal of thought and effort . . . if you know of anyone who likes Dostoievsky or Knut Hamsun . . . they will thoroughly appreciate *Brass.*"³⁵ While, in *Brass,* Norris does not reach the towering heights of Dostoevsky, he certainly shares a respectable level with the Norwegian novelist, Hamsun.

Bread: The Plot

Bread's central character, unlike those in Norris's three previous novels, is a woman. Jeannette Sturgis, elder daughter of a widowed piano teacher and professional accompanist, resents her family's frugal existence enough to seek an early independence. The teenage Jeannette graduates first in her secretarial class and secures a job in a publishing house that allows her mother and younger sister, Alice, to share in her increased comfort and security.

Jeannette is infatuated with her fellow employee, Roy Beardsley, but, rather than giving up her job and independence to housewifery, she promotes the marriage of Roy and Alice. Her job with the house president, Chandler B. Corey, comes even before her love for the dashingly handsome young salesman, Martin Devlin. Jeannette marries Martin only after the prospects of a scandal, prompted by false rumors circulated by Corey's jealous wife, threaten embarrassment for her boss.

The marriage to Martin, devoted and loving but a spendthrift, proves a mixed blessing to a woman who remains obsessed with money and harbors nostalgia for her independence. When Martin continues to gamble with their modest income and press her for a child she is reluctant to have, Jeannette leaves him for her former job. Now free from any hint of scandal, she gradually rises to the highest position available to a woman of her talents. Jeannette grows troubled by the near vacuum in her life beyond her position as head of the company mailroom. At forty-three, some fifteen years after her separation from Martin, she seeks him out. Her discovery that he had secured a hasty divorce seven years earlier and married a handsome widow with three children is numbing. The novel's last scene shows Jeannette in her bachelor apartment, half consumed with regret and bitterness, seeking solace from a sole companion, her pet cat.

More Savor

Bread received a majority of favorable reviews. It also sold well. The *New York Times Book Review,* on 19 August 1923, sounded the keynote: "Norris has added several cubits to his stature by sheer application. . . . He is not . . . a good writer, but he has made himself a good novelist, one who improves at each effort."[36] Four months later *Booklist,* on 23 December 1923, applauded the novel's logical development and Norris's "progress in . . . style and workmanship."[37] Earlier, on 18 August 1923, the *Boston Evening Transcript* had praised him for "a reality that is extraordinarily truthful . . . a very fine story . . . a genuine transcript of real life." The rather squeamish reviewer saw *Bread* as (happily) "without the slightest sugges- tion of an effort to follow in the naturalistic footsteps of Zola . . . strikingly frank and vigorous in its detail of a woman's life from youth to middle age . . . faithfully recorded with the eye of the photographer and the brush of the artist."[38]

Referring to this "gray recital that outdoes Schopenhauer," that is not so much the work of "an artist as a reporter," aiming "at literalness not literary quality," Isabel Paterson of the *New York Tribune News and Review,* on 19 August 1923, declared *Bread* "a really admirable piece of work," even though it "goes off target."[39] Robert Morss Lovett, writing for the *New Republic* on 29 August 1923, was a bit backhanded with his compli- ments: "Of his . . . novels *Bread* is undoubtedly the best, partly because Mr. Norris has been fortunate in his selections of theme and background. . . . although the narrative never breaks the speed laws . . . it never gets lost. The style is without a single gleam of brilliance or distinction but it avoids the egregious platitudes of *Brass*."[40] In a review with feminist overtones Louise Maunsell Field of the *Literary Digest Interna- tional Book Review,* on 23 September 1923, favored both the "message" and Norris's execution of it, although she thought that the book intended "as a protest against women in business [was] in truth an arraignment of men in general. . . ."[41] H. M. Boynton (writing for the *Independent* on 29 September 1923) saw "reality in the central idea and fidelity in much of the detail. . . ." While to Boynton the prose was "stodgy," it was also "carefully written."[42] The *Springfield Sunday Republican* saw "the storyteller and the propagandist struggling for mastery" in a novel that is nonetheless "soundly based and developed with no little artistry . . . a narrative capable of giving enjoyment and commanding the reader's interest."[43]

The *Dial*, less than enthusiastic in "Briefer Mention," on 28 November 1923, accused *Bread* of "a style as formless as an amoeba" and of emulating "the specious exactitude of Sinclair Lewis and the mania of Upton Sinclair for persecuting maladjustments. . . . an indiscriminatingly voluble slave of the realistic school. . . . [Norris] has dedicated an egregiously drab book to the proposition that existence is a bad business."[44] A more thoughtful review (and a more favorable one) in *Current Opinion*, October 1923, talked of the "almost startling conservatism of . . . *Bread* . . . a book that sets itself squarely against . . . the advancing tide of feminism. . . ."[45] After a few gastronomical metaphors, the *Nation*, October 1923, settled down to qualified approval: "one wishes that the novelist had been willing to discard a little more, retaining only the essentials of his otherwise interesting and well-composed novel, which deals sanely with the problem of women in business and its bearing upon marriage."[46] Ruth Snyder, writing on 7 October 1923 for the *New York World*, responded to the novel with favor only after she had given a rave notice to Kathleen's *Butterfly*, published by Doubleday the same month Doran released *Bread*. She particularly liked Kathleen's "interpretation of women," wishing that she would teach Charles the "art of tactfulness," lamenting that his characters, "although good," have not "the finesse of our Kathleen. . . ." Berating Charles for having "both attacked and defended the business woman," she still called *Bread* "by far [his] best literary work. . . ."[47]

Both Paterson and Field responded to what seemed to them in *Bread* a mixture of irony and contradiction. Paterson claimed that "Feminists . . . are liable to break into a rash or irritation, unless they take this story with . . . irony. My sole perplexity

. . . is to decide whether or not Mr. Norris meant to supply the irony. . . ." She further claimed that, in regard to Devlin's second marriage, "Mr. Norris wrote with his tongue in his cheek, poking sly fun at the happy-ending convention. On the other hand, business is depicted as a dreary sort of treadmill wherein women need never hope for justice or equitable treatment."[48] To Field, Norris practically "declare[s] that a man must depend mainly on his wife's financial need to prevent her from leaving him," which she sees as "being decidedly severe on the man."[49] The concluding paragraph of the *New York Times* review attempted to deal with the issue of authorial intention in *Bread:*

> Since it seems to be the function of the American novel to convey a message, . . . a moral lesson could easily be drawn from the story of Jeannette Sturgis; but only the old and somewhat hackneyed one that you can't eat your cake and have it too, and even that is not universally valid. There ought to be general satisfaction over the prospective demise of Preacher Norris and the prospective continuation of Novelist Norris. America is full of novelists able to say the last word on questions which had remained unsettled until the coming of the enlightened age, but there are not many who can so surely catch the feeling of business life and the relation of business workers to the machine.[50]

Woman's Dilemma

Whatever Norris's purpose, *Bread* is very much a woman's book. Although his portrayal of Jeannette is not altogether favorable, it is almost always sympathetic. His dedication of *Bread* "To the Working Women of America" is more feminist than ironic. Jeannette's plight is that of a second-class citizen, trapped in a male-oriented world that has helped to form her ambivalent attitude toward marriage and children. The more successful marriage of Alice and Roy (undercut somewhat by shallow domesticity) provides another framework for her failed marriage and mutedly successful business career. Despite a certain naiveté and ineffectuality, Alice and Roy (as do Rosemary and Harry in *Brass*) become an embodiment of the value of hard work enhanced by the love of children. A home and children are, on the other hand, all that Alice ever wanted. She had neither Jeannette's desire nor her talent for the business world. Norris again avoids an easy solution to a complex issue.

There are the usual biographical parallels in *Bread* to Charles's and Kathleen's lives. At the end of the novel, for instance, Jeannette at forty-three is the same age as Norris. Her purchase of tickets to *Parsifal* at the Met is directly out of Norris's life. The newly married Devlins enjoy the same activities that Charles and Kathleen so enjoyed during the first year of their marriage:

> Nights on which they did not go to the theatre, they roamed the bright upper stretches of Broadway, sauntered along Riverside Drive as far as Grant's Tomb, or meandered into the Park, where electric lights cast a theatrical radiance on trees and shrubbery. On Sundays they made excursions to the beaches, and one week-end they went to Coney Island on Saturday afternoon and stayed the night at the Manhattan Beach Hotel. Jeannette long remembered the glorious planked steak they enjoyed for dinner . . . , sitting at a little table by the porch railing, listening to the big military band, while all about them a gay throng chatted and laughed at other tables, and crowds surged up and down the boardwalk as the Atlantic thundered a dull rhythmical bourdon to the stirring music of trumpet and drum.[51]

Devlin's Friday night poker game is a scaled down version of Charles's own weekly affairs. And the "Wonderful day" at the beach the Devlins share with the Beardsleys is a faithful recapturing of idyllic picnics the Norrises shared with the Benéts before World War I (320–28). Jeannette shares Kathleen's amusement over solitaire and when Alice and Roy go west to California, it is to the Mill Valley of Kathleen's youth.

Traces of Frank Norris's influence are no stranger to *Bread.* The heroine's first name is that of Frank's wife; her last name echoes that of one of Frank's pseudonyms, Justin Sturgis, used when he was writing for the *Wave.* Again Charles is partial to his brother's penchant for triplets in his descriptive passages, as in his description of one of Jeannette's bosses: "Mr. Edmund was the Napoleon, the Great King, the Far-seeing Master . . ." (50). There are striking parallels to Frank Norris's treatment of adultery. Regarding the flirtation of the rich playboy, "idler and trifler" Gerald Kenyon with Jeannette, Charles writes: "The incident that stirred his [Martin's] memory was the chance

discovery of two cigarette stubs in a little glass ashtray. . . .
Jeannette did not smoke" (354). In regard to Laura Jadwin's
affair with the dilletantish bachelor Lane Corthell in *The Pit,*
Frank had used a similar touch. Besides noticing Corthell's
heartshaped matchbox in Laura's private sittingroom, Page (her
sister) observes that "'He was here, . . . long enough to smoke
half a dozen times.' She pointed to a silver pen tray . . . littered
with the ashes and charred stumps of some five or six cigarettes."[52] Laura, too, is a nonsmoker. There are also strong
parallels between the moments of sexual submission of Jeannette and Trina McTeague; Trina's pecunious nature has left its
mark on Jeannette.

Perhaps the most notable aspect of *Bread,* however, is
Norris's treatment of the predicament of the professional
woman in the male-dominated business world between the
1890s and World War I. Job hunting early in her career,
Jeannette is treated as a sex object by those in power: "Twice
Jeannette had the unpleasant experience of having men to
whom she had applied for work lay their hands on her. One
slipped his arm about her, and tried to kiss her, pressing a wet
mustache against her face; the other placed his fat fingers
caressingly over hers, leering at her, promised he would find
her a good job, if she'd come back later in the day. She was
equal to the occasions but there was always a sickening reaction
that left her weak and trembling with a salt taste in her mouth.
She said nothing about them at home" (99–100).

Norris presents a myriad of stereotypical antifeminist view-
points, usually choosing the least sympathetic characters to
express these prejudices, always making it clear that he himself
believes that "she [Jeannette] was cleverer than most men"
(56). Two of her superiors at the publishing company object to
her promotion to head of the mail-order department even after
she has proved her abilities for many years as Mr. Corey's
executive secretary: "Mr. Kipps and Mr. Featherstone shared
the opinion that a woman was not competent to manage affairs
involving so much money,—they were too large for the feminine mind to grasp" (394). They warn Corey that "he was in
great danger of demoralizing [the company] by permitting a *girl*
to assume its management" (394). Jeannette makes far less
money than did her male predecessor at the same job. Again

Kipps attempts to justify such inequality: "it would never do to pay women employees more than fifty dollars a week; they wouldn't know what to do with the money" (457). The easy fortune of a former Corey employer who was now "one of the big men in Sears Roebuck and Company" gives Jeannette more reason to object. Exasperated, she, who "felt herself to be cleverer than he, more able in every respect," watches him get "ten thousand—twelve thousand—fifteen thousand . . . a year and climbing the ladder of success rung after rung, while she was doing the work he had left behind him at the Corey Publishing Company in a far more efficient, economical, and profitable way and was paid fifty dollars a week!" (399–400). Her limited success comes only after "a long struggle. . . . Mr. Kipps . . . had hampered her in every way he could . . . because she was a woman and he had no faith in a woman's judgment" (395). This sexist view persists long after Jeannette has proved herself as Corey's right-hand woman. Norris makes her abilities very clear: "Mr. Corey respected her judgment, frequently consulted her and sometimes followed her advice even when contrary to his inclinations" (223).

Given her history of comparatively low salaries, it is understandable that money would become an obsession with her. At one point, when her first fiancé longs for kisses, her attention is elsewhere: "Just now she wanted Roy to help her guess the salaries of everyone in the office" (129). At another point she listens with envy to Roy's talk of office politics and camaraderie: "Jeannette studied her lover's face and for a moment felt actual dislike for him. . . . Why should *he* be so fortunate? Why should everything go so smoothly for *him?* Why shouldn't *she* have a chance like that?" (102). Later, as head of the "Mail Order Department," she matches her ambition with creativity: "It was a pet idea of hers that women, not men, bought books by mail and she was confident that attacks directed at women, written from a feminine standpoint, would show results. . . . She had great confidence in herself . . . and was sure she could increase sales and manage the department better than Walt Chase. . . . she had played secretary long enough . . . she wanted her chance at bigger work" (393). Her ideas are successful; she is better at the job than Chase was. Her success makes her earlier frustrations at going from salaried employee to housewife even clearer: "What part of his weekly paycheck was [Devlin] likely to give her to run their house, and to spend on herself? . . . the question of the wife's allowance in marriage seemed a vital one to her" (219).

By the end of the novel Jeannette has been so demoralized during much of her limited career as bachelor businesswoman that she has reversed her stance and adopted an antifeminist view to spare her eighteen-year-old niece from similar unhappiness: "The more I live, the more I am convinced that women have no place in business. . . . The country is being deprived of homes and children because of the great invasion of women into business during the last twenty or thirty years. . . . since man is intended by God and Nature to be the worker, and woman is ordained to bear children . . . women have no place in the business world" (464–65). She has not only become a mouthpiece for masculine supremacy in business but has, sadly, canonized her own unfulfilled maternal instincts. Norris leaves Jeannette in a predicament that is partially society's fault, partially her own. Her ultimate dissatisfaction, together with the bittersweet scenes of summer holidays on Long Island beaches, look forward to scenes in Norris's next novel of rags to (this time) riches. Sam Smith of *Pig Iron* is in many ways the male counterpart of Jeannette Sturgis.

Merits

Even though most of the critics liked *Bread,* it is generally a weaker novel than either *Salt* or *Brass*. Nevertheless, Norris has left a valuable document on women's rights. George Creel, the Norrises' good friend, volunteered an assessment of *Bread* that remains sound. On 17 October 1923 he wrote to Charles:

The average modern novel not only wastes your time at the time, but induces a habit of careless reading that is all too sadly in evidence when a worth-while book comes along. I have not written before because I gulped "Bread" at first and had to go over it again to get the full good of it. I thought that "Salt" was the best thing of its day, "Brass" made equal appeal to me, and now I have the same conviction with regard to "Bread." It is not only a big thing that you have done, but an important thing, for it deals with life as it is being lived—

brilliantly, intimately, interpretatively and helpfully. What I like best about your craft is that you are able to make people think without the slightest sacrifice of narrative value, for "Bread" is as entertaining as stimulating. Go on and on, old boy, just as you have done, refusing to make shabby compromises that have ruined so many of our most promising writers.[53]

Chapter Four
Pig Iron and *Zelda Marsh*

Pig Iron: The Story

Pig Iron traces Samuel Osgood Smith's life from his birth (the day General Lee surrendered at Appomatox) in 1865 until his sixtieth year in 1925, the middle of the postwar boom. After years of hard work on their Massachusetts farm culminate in the deaths of his parents, he seeks his fortune at twenty in New York City. There he lives with his pious, good-hearted Uncle Cyrus and Aunt Sarah. With the help of a hypocritical but charitable Sunday school teacher, Baldwin Wright, Sam gets a job as a stock boy at the Atlas Nail and Wire Company. Baldwin Wright's bachelor apartment, where young men gather for beer, snacks, and literary readings, is the site of Sam's introduction to his lifelong friends: Jack Cheney, a very bright and agreeable medical student primed for a successful career; Vin Morrisey, a brilliant wit who will become an itinerant author, painter, and adventurer; and Taylor Evans, a talented writer who will move from critical to popular success as a novelist.

During one of the more lively evenings on the town with these young men Sam falls in love with Evelyn, a prostitute, and lives with her for a year before she leaves him to join a traveling road show. Heartbroken and ill with pneumonia, he recuperates slowly. His aunt's and uncle's forgiveness helps him channel his energies into business, and he becomes enchanted by success. Sam rides a bicycle to rural stores bypassed by other salesmen, and with help from his wealthy brother-in-law (Phineas Holliday, husband of his sister Narcissa) and the cooperation of his boss (Mr. Faber), he follows many of the precepts of the Horatio Alger formula, including marrying the boss's daughter (Paula Faber).

Marriage to Paula gradually becomes unsatisfactory, as she pursues her pseudo-artistic endeavors and he loses himself in the speculative world of high finance. At the novel's end the sixty-year-old Samuel Osgood Smith (who has taken care of his first love, Evelyn, with monthly checks) sits alienated from his slight son (who should have been born a girl) and large daughter (who is more hoydenish than girlish). He hears a distress call on the radio, his only remaining source of amusement.

The Reactions

The reviews of *Pig Iron* were overwhelmingly favorable. Doran gave it considerably more promotion than Scribner's gave to a novel published at exactly the same time, *The Great Gatsby*. It outsold *Gatsby* as well as Dos Passos's *Manhattan Transfer* and Dreiser's *An American Tragedy*, two other novels of 1925. The most negative reviewers among a very small group who attacked Norris's fifth novel included, once more, Robert Morss Lovett of the *New Republic*, on 21 April, 1926 and the anonymous reviewer for *Booklist*, on 23 June 1926, who had praised *Bread* less than three years before. Lovett's one-paragraph review is mostly plot summary sandwiched between his analogical remarks: "Mr. Norris's novels remind us of concrete roads, accurately surveyed and exactly executed according to specifications to stand the wear and tear of heavy traffic. . . . but the milestones tend to make us conscious of the slowness of the pace. We feel like pedestrians on an automobile road, and become footsore before the end."[1] *Booklist*'s conclusion is terser, pronouncing the novel "without humor or brilliance."[2] The favorable reviewers saw solid value in *Pig Iron*, and some of them treated Norris as a major novelist, comparing him favorably with his brother and with Dreiser.

Joseph Wood Krutch's review for the *Saturday Review of Literature*, 6 March 1926, presented the majority report aptly:

The idea of turning the Alger books wrong side out seems to have occurred to Mr. Dreiser and Mr. Norris at about the same time . . . : Mr. Norris is no satirist and no cynic; he scoffs at nothing . . . but he manages . . . to point out the spiritual barrenness of the period which ended with the Great War.

Denied as he is either humor or brilliance Mr. Norris is nevertheless able to demand the respect and hold the interest of his readers by virtue of a certain dogged seriousness of mind. . . . Mr. Norris cannot describe a tragedy with Dreiser's exultant ferocity. . . . Yet he has withal the gift of creating a solid and convincing background. Granted an intense conviction or a glowing passion his writings would be great; as it is they are no more than honestly good.[3]

The *American Mercury* (1926) added a supportive footnote: "His novels . . . have received a great deal less critical attention than they deserve. . . . What he sets forth he knows. . . . His books have a solid substance in them and a fine dignity."[4] Stuart Sherman of the *New York Herald Tribune Books*, on 14 March 1926, declared that "There is a large place in American fiction for Charles G. Norris,"[5] a conviction supported by the claim of the *Literary Digest International Book Review* that "Mr. Norris has done by far his best and most important work. . . . *Pig Iron* has many of the defects and merits of Dreiser. . . . The writing, however, has a grace of sentence that is free from the turgid lapses of Dreiser."[6] To the *Nation and Athenaeum,* on 4 September 1928, Charles's "talent recalls Zola's genius. Both are thorough, sincere, competent and interesting, even when they are most tedious. . . . Mr. Norris is unlike Zola, in that, although he writes fairly sound prose (admitting numerous blemishes), his style has poetic intensity." The reviewer hastened to add that (unlike Zola) "He is never offensive."[7] The *London Times Literary Supplement* for 26 August 1926 continued its support of Charles's work: "[*Pig Iron*] is very long, very carefully written and maintained on a fine sense of irony . . . [with a] beautifully ironic ending."[8] Even the *Dial* for October 1926 was won over by *Pig Iron,* calling it "a novel of solid and authentic worth." The reviewer applauded Norris's handling of "his favorite theme—the effects of industrialism upon human relationships" with "greater breadth than ever before."[9]

It was Francis Edwin Edgett and John W. Crawford, however, who sounded the most resonant representative notes. Edgett in the 6 March 1926 *Boston Evening Transcript* saw "a noble portrait of Sam Smith's mother" in a novel that is "a long story, but . . . does not seem too long. . . . Seldom has there appeared a novel that combines with the story so vigorous and so sincere a study of humanity. The two are wedded inextricably

into a masterly piece of fiction."[10] Crawford's commentary in
"Norris Portrays the Steel Age," in the *New York World* for 7
March 1926, was, if somewhat less laudatory, a more penetrat-
ing assessment. Since his essay summarizes the remarks of at
least a dozen highly favorable reviews, I will quote it at length.
After praising the "character of Sam Osgood Smith," which is
"developed as Theodore Dreiser elaborates Clyde Griffith,"
and commending Norris's selectivity of detail and his focus on
"aspects of people and events which . . ." achieve "an illusion of
identification with Sam," Crawford makes his central points
about Sam's characterization, how Norris presents him "with
sympathy but without sentimentality":

Almost imperceptibly the fresh, open, direct youth has turned into
a man of a single idea. Mr. Norris contrives the transition very
skillfully. Sam is a personified will-to-get-rich.
   The concluding picture of Sam as the respected and feared million-
aire maintaining an outward show of the conjugal relation which his
wife has been ignoring for years, fathering the alien and ill-assorted
children, finding solace only in the radio—that Sam is an ironical
commentary on his younger self.
   Pig Iron . . . is a sober, sensible man's visualization of spiritual
values, or their absence, in the steel age. The novel draws aside the
veil of romance about . . . the self-made millionaire, that legendary
figure, part genius, part pirate, wholly glamorous, and shows him for
what he is—a grubbing, fanatical opportunist.[11]

Sources

Autobiographical traces are once again quite evident in *Pig
Iron*. Samuel Osgood Smith's parents, like Gertrude Doggett
Norris's, are "Americans on both sides right down from
Colonial days."[12] Sam's father's (Theophilus Smith's) love of
English poetry and the classics recalls both Gertrude's and
Kathleen's father's love of literature, just as Theophilus's
"Young Ladies Seminary" recalls the school Gertrude's brother
ran before the Civil War. Theophilus's farm in Mendon,
Massachusetts, is very much like the Doggett homestead in
Taunton. Charles is recalling the imaginative games he and
Frank played with toy soldiers when he describes the Smith
children "Playing with baby-chinks . . . [telling] extravagantly

fantastic stories that were woven around the various personalities with which these 'dressed rags' were endowed" (9). As in Kathleen's own tragic experience, the Smith children lose both their parents: "Twice within the space of three short weeks death struck . . ." (45). Sam is almost exactly the same age Kathleen was when death struck twice at Treehaven in Mill Valley. Charles also drew from both B. F. Norris and the fictional Curtis Jadwin of *The Pit* for Baldwin Wright's enthusiastic role as a Sunday school teacher. But the character who reflects the most specific biographical parallels draws the major part of his attributes and activities from Charles's brother Frank. Vin Morrisey is, as was Frank Norris, an artist, poet, photographer, and adventurer. Like Frank he visited South Africa and involved himself both in the abortive Jameison raid on Johannesburg during the Boer War and in the invasion of Cuba during the Spanish American War. The account of Paula's difficult second labor and exhausting recovery was written from Charles's vivid memories of Kathleen's difficult time during and after the infant death of their twin daughters. Sam's serious financial setback is suffused with the knowledge Charles gleaned from his own business ventures and the near bankruptcy of Jadwin in *The Pit*.

The literary echoes and allusions in *Pig Iron* seem stronger than ever. Even the minor characters owe debts to Frank's novels. Narcissa's early love, Nick ("No one ever knew where Nick came from"), is as memorably ignominious as the loner Dabney in *The Octopus* (26). The major characters often act in like manner. Both Annixter (of *The Octopus)* and Sam kick dogs to vent jealous frustration. Similar in build as well as in eating habits to Frank's McTeague, the youthful Sam "ate hugely and grossly the food that was set before him" (27). Sex to young Sam, as to many of Frank's characters (especially McTeague and Vandover), is purely "animal desire" (32). Paula curling in Sam's lap and calling him her "bear" reminds one of Trina in McTeague's lap pulling his bearlike head toward her by his ears. The pressures on Evelyn and Sam to economize by moving to cheaper quarters parallel Trina's and McTeague's actual moves. And again such small details as the memory-laden scent permeating Sam's dead father's clothes recalls the nostalgia-ridden odor of hair oil on the hat of Vandover's deceased father.

Reminiscent of Frank's sensory-filled novels, *Pig Iron* is filled with "the smell of perspiration, cigarettes, sachet perfume and food mingled" with "noise-color-movement-movement-color-noise" (127). Sam's queasy experience in church the morning after his drunken orgy recalls Vandover's drunken visit to church that ends with his kneeling at the communion rail fighting a churning stomach. The play rehearsal scene in which Sam is a reluctant amateur participant (97–98) mirrors the rehearsal scene in *The Pit,* during which a prima donna of a director badgers an amateur actress to tears. Ruth speaks out for the humiliated Sam in the same manner that Laura defends the young lady. Paula's young suitor, Richard Dorn, is a near composite of Landry Court and Lane Corthell in their courtship of Laura Dearborn. Another of Paula's suitors, Gordon Detweiler, provides the context for a contrast of business and the arts (361–62) and covers essentially the same ground as do Corthell and Laura with Jadwin. There is also a clear parallel between phases of Sam's career and Jadwin's. In *Pig Iron,* "The next three years were exciting, unsettled. In them Sam turned gambler. . . . Little by little he was drawn into the habit of speculating" (355). This is an almost exact description of Jadwin's bear and bull years. Sam's refusal to touch his wife's personal bonds when destruction threatens is also Jadwin's. The novelist Taylor Evans's *Miranda of the Tenements* is a takeoff on Crane's *Maggie, A Girl of the Streets.* Sam's power to "compel men to do his bidding" (266) is the same as Dreiser's Frank Cowperwood's. And Sam's belief that "The whole world was based on the theory of the big fellow eating the little fellow" (361) is almost identical to both Cowperwood's lobster/squid philosophy and Jadwin's monomaniacal disregard of the little fellow in the name of success-at-all-cost.

Standing the Test

On the surface *Pig Iron* seems another typical rags-to-riches story filled with undertones of Horatio Alger. But from the outset Norris undercuts the American dream of material success. Theophilus Smith's hard work leads him nowhere but the grave. The Horatio Alger pep talk from Baldwin Wright to Sam (newly arrived to the city from the country) proves an ironic

comment on the American Dream. For Wright, like many
businessmen who aspire to success, is corrupt and dishonest,
eventually caught with his hand in the Sunday school till.
Although he uses some of the stolen money to help his young
men, the rest supports Wright's own comfortable life-style. The
undercurrent of possibly homosexual vibrations between Baldwin Wright and Adrian Lane, one of his protégés and the
recipient of financial as well as emotional support, leads to
Wright's "utter demoralization" (118) and eventual suicide. His
chicanery surfaces near the beginning of the novel in the lies he
is willing to tell on Sam's behalf to secure him his job. He
chooses expediency and self-indulgence over morality.

If Norris's ironic attitude toward immorality in business is
one-sided, his attitude toward Sam himself is not. It is clearly
ambivalent. At the end, money, success, and power have not
bought Sam happiness. His happiest times (often fleeting ones)
are during the acquisition of wealth and status, and throughout
most of his bittersweet love affair with Evelyn the year before
his successful career begins. John Crawford is exactly right
when he describes Norris's treatment of Sam's love affair with
Evelyn as "one of sympathy without sentimentality."[13]

Norris also handles Sam's marriage of compromise very well,
as he traces the indifference gradually consuming the marriage
and supplanting it with flashes of jealousy and hatred. There is a
psychological validity in Sam's becoming best friends with
Paula's intimate, Matt Madison, the man who should gather his
most virulent resentment. Sam's progressive alienation from
Paula and his movement toward a truce, a compromise, are
deftly handled. The gradual shifts in their sleeping arrange-
ments speak for themselves. On their wedding night it is Sam's
preoccupation with business that prompts his late arrival at
their single bed. Paula is already asleep. A few years later Sam
quietly notes the significance of Paula's introduction of twin
beds when she is furnishing their new apartment. Still later, in
their mansion, Paula makes sure that Sam has "his own room"
(408).

Unlike Griffith Adams of *Salt,* but very much like Philip
Baldwin of *Brass,* Sam finds neither sustained happiness nor
contentment. Nor does he ultimately discover it in the lives of
the friends he most admired in his youth. Sam's sentimental

journey (at fifty-eight) to visit Jack Cheney and Vin Morrisey shows him that their lives are no more enviable than his own. Cheney is a plodding general practitioner in the Midwest. Morrisey lives a glamorless life in an adobe hut in Arizona. In their lives he sees none of the happiness that had eluded him. Taylor Evans has sold out for money. Evelyn, the source of his greatest happiness, dies three days before their long-anticipated reunion. Sam's closest remaining friend, Matt Madison, dies half-destroyed by Paula's cruel treatment of him.

The "Rosebud" ending (with Evelyn's ragdoll as a vague counterpart to Charles Foster Kane's sled in Orson Welles's movie) is better prepared for and more appropriate than the final scene in *Bread* that leaves Jeannette Sturgis with only a cat for comfort. Alone with this toy memento of almost forty years, drowned in nostalgia and listening to a ship's distress signal on the radio—a signal which ironically and appropriately spells out his initials, Sam can salvage no vestiges of his youthful joys. The happiness of his year with Evelyn and the hours of childhood play with his own toy "dressed rags" are only memories. Like Charlie Wales of Fitzgerald's "Babylon Revisited," he turns to the dead for comfort, and does so in vain.

The reader who has shared most of Sam's six decades with him is left feeling compassionate. The author has managed to elicit these feelings by creating a real character in a real world. Along with his insights into the life of a businessman during the robber baron days, he has provided the reader, in his authentic descriptions of New York of the 1880s and 1890s, with the businessman's day-to-day world. From Sam's third-floor window on the night of his arrival in the city:

Occasionally laughter could be heard and there was a constant low babble of voices and now and then a woman's highpitched tone. Down in the dark of the double row of yards on the stoops outside the kitchens and underneath the thick screening foliage of sheltering trees, gossip and love-making were going on. The night smelled of hot tin roofs cooling, of tar, of dry ashes and stale cooking. Men and women in various stages of undress appeared and disappeared at uncurtained windows, and where the shades were drawn, now and then a giant shadow was thrown upon the screen with huge distorted arms and hands. At some distance a cornetist practiced mournfully while from the street a hurdy-gurdy added its merry twinkle. (54)

Norris's descriptions chart the growing sophistication of Sam at the same time that they detail his environment, as in the descriptions of the home of his future father-in-law:

Sam had not visited the Faber home since the day he had gone there, a red-handed brawny stock-room boy, to help move furniture. . . . There lingered in his mind a recollection of polished marquetried floors, of satin-covered chairs, and glass cabinets filled with rare and beautiful bric-a-brac, of golden framed oil paintings and rich brocades at the windows, the shining ebony luster of the piano reflecting soft and colorful lights. The piano still stood in one corner, the glass cabinets still ranged themselves against the walls, and on the floor was spread the same white polar bear rug with its enormous head and red gaping mouth. But now the rare and beautiful bric-a-brac behind the doors of the glass cabinets seemed insignificant, a collection of unimportant shells and trash, the pictures dull and uninteresting, the polished hardwood floor had cracked and lost its gloss, the bear rug looked clumsy, the piano, old-fashioned, the brocaded curtains musty and voluminous. (267–68)

The dramatic changes in Sam's perception of the Faber living quarters also prefigures his disillusionment with the Faber daughter and his marriage to her. His love will fade like these furnishings and become as moribund as the piano upon which a beautiful but aloof Paula first played so pretentiously.

Pig Iron's thematically controlled descriptive details provide the appropriately shifting realistic backdrop for one of Charles Norris's most successful characters. It is mainly what he has made of Samuel Osgood Smith that makes *Pig Iron* one of Charles's three best novels.

Zelda Marsh: Cinderella

In one of several flashbacks in *Zelda Marsh,* the reader learns that Zelda's only memories of her deceased mother are fond but vague ones of being cradled by a "sweet-faced, soft-cheeked" woman. Her pleasantest memories with her father, Joe Marsh, "an itinerant cook," are of her "happy and exciting" days when he cooked for a circus. "In her eighteenth year Zelda could truthfully say that the most intense emotion she had ever known was her love" for "a white woolly lamb."[14] Her half-blind father had been forced to send her to live in the strict household of her Uncle Caleb and Aunt Mary Burgess.

Zelda is more at home in her imagination than in their comfortably conservative two-story house of the frame construction typical of "nearly every residence in San Francisco during the early nineties." She would rather dream romantic dreams in the greenhouse or the "sizable and rather pretty garden" than do her schoolwork (2).

At seventeen she falls in love with a sixteen-year-old classmate, Michael Kirk, son of her neighbor and music teacher, who discovers them consummating their love in Michael's makeshift artist's studio. The Burgesses' threats to commit Zelda to St. Catherine's school to live as a virtual prisoner send her to her uncle's chess partner, Dr. Boylston, who hides her in his medical offices where she stays, eventually as his mistress, for two years. She leaves Boylston after Mrs. Kirk has frustrated her attempts to win Michael back by taking her son to Paris. Stage experience with a San Francisco theatrical troupe ignites her ambition for a stage career in New York City.

In a New York theatrical rooming house Zelda meets the shy John Harney and confesses her past. A juvenile romantic actor, George Selby, convinces her to overlook his drinking and gambling in deference to his good looks and charm and marry him. They tour in a vaudeville skit. Within a year Zelda has gained theatrical and marital experience, had an abortion, and, because a flirtation with a childhood admirer, Jerry Page, discloses her past, has lost an angry husband. She survives infection from the abortion after three months in a San Francisco hospital, borrows money for a ticket to New York, and secures a job as housekeeper at her old roominghouse.

She cannot long resist the temptations of the stage, however, and before long has triumphed in her first Broadway play. John, realizing his own love is hopeless, introduces her to his wealthy nephew and playwright, Tom Harney, who falls in love with Zelda and writes a play for her. *The Drudge* brings Zelda fame, adoration, and money. Marriage to Tom is close when first Michael then George appear (both down and almost out) to complicate her happy existence. After the shock of George's drunken suicide which follows her rejection of him, Zelda takes Michael to a tuberculosis sanitorium in Arizona to ease his final days. She leaves the door open for Tom Harney, just a crack, by telling John that if Tom still loves her "tell him to come and find me" (486).

Reception

In their responses to *Zelda Marsh* reviewers again praised Norris's details and again linked his name with Dreiser's, but no one seemed terribly enthusiastic about his sixth novel. Edwin Clark's remarks, in the *New York Times Book Review* for 14 August 1927, were typical of the reception of what he called a rewritten "tale of Cinderella," a "romance decked out in the guise of realistic fiction." According to Clark, although Norris has "frequently . . . treated youthful love with sympathy and insight," the novel is "all only half real with cleverly devised pleas for sympathy and utterly unintelligible motivation." He was just as unhappy with the "contrived final scene that is the equal of the hectic looseness of the narrative."[15] While she thought that "coincidence has a long reach" in *Zelda Marsh,* Ruth Burr Sanborn of the *New York Herald Tribune,* on 28 August 1927, was happier with Norris's talent for drawing men whom "we cannot admire—and cannot help liking," and concluded with bland approval that "Mr. Norris has written a novel worth writing."[16] Ernest Southerland Bates's review in the *Saturday Review of Literature,* on 17 September 1927, was more neutral. He acknowledged that "Mr. Norris has succeeded in making Zelda's fascination over . . . men she meets perfectly plausible. . . . Zelda moves out of the story triumphant and into our memories." He was somewhat puzzled by Norris's quotation from Philip Massinger on the title page ("Virtue is but a word / Fortune rules all"): "Is Mr. Norris himself taken in by the heroics of his heroine at the end of the book? . . . the prospect of a happy love [is] quickly terminated by one of those sets of quixotic renunciation which the world calls noble." Bates asked: "is the quotation an ironic comment on the story? Or is the story an ironic comment on the quotation?"[17]

The one-paragraph review in the *Nation,* on 2 November 1927, was unfavorable but not exactly sanguinary: "Mr. Norris, following in the wake of the popular interest in stage folk, offers the turgid tale of Zelda who proves her basic virtue despite several transgressions of the Seventh Commandment, by returning to her first lover and seducer in his time of need."[18] The phrase "popular interest" may better describe Charles's target than the excitement generated by his result. Perhaps certain affinities with Kathleen's tamer versions of this more risqué brand of "Cinderella" story distracted reviewers.

The *Commonweal* reviewer, on 7 December 1927, may have spelled out what others greeted with puzzlement: "In concocting the adventures of *Zelda Marsh,* Charles G. Norris has taken a sabbatical year from his serious studies of the American scene. He has turned from the novel to romance." And although the reviewer also praised Norris, it was not for particularly exciting intellectual achievements: "There are . . . some pretty sketches of New York and theatrical life during the gas-light and heavy plush age. The account of a vaudeville tour is also interesting."[19]

Possibly because it is closer to Kathleen Norris's romances than are his other novels, more derivative of a specific genre, there are few traces of autobiographical influences and parallels in *Zelda Marsh.* In the possessiveness of Mrs. Kirk toward Michael and his art career there is a hint of Gertrude Norris's dedication to Frank, but there similarities between the women vanish. Mrs. Harney in her devotion to her son Tom is a sympathetic version of Gertrude. The names of stores in Zelda's old Polk Street and Van Ness neighborhood also came from Charles's own memories. Nor could he resist an inside joke on one of his many nicknames. During George Selby's account of his life after his separation from Zelda, he mentions having "made a hit in that old has-been [The Mikado], play[ing] 'Poohbah'" (441).

The Art

Literary debts and echoes are more apparent than those biographical. Again the works of Frank Norris and Theodore Dreiser are among his sources. George and Zelda's wedding is performed with background distractions even more discordant and foreboding than the persistent sound of sawing during the ceremony of the McTeagues: "A fire engine, its bell clanging furiously went racketing up Fifth Avenue" and then "Another bell, a high shrilling, silvery note" (175). Just as McTeague seems comical stuffed into his wedding suit, "George looked so funny in that tight cutaway." Zelda's "hooking" of George's change and her hoarding of it are milder symptoms of what becomes Trina McTeague's obsession. The leavening influence of Tom Harney's artistic creativity on Zelda is a variation on Robert Ames's heightening of Carrie's aesthetic awareness. And in their poverty and desperation, Michael and George (especially) share attributes with Dreiser's George Hurstwood as he descends to suicide. While Carrie, absorbed in her theatrical world, is oblivious to Hurstwood's despair, Zelda, unable to save Selby, manages at least to prolong Michael's life at the expense of her career. There are stronger parallels, however, between Zelda's second meeting with Selby after his return and Carrie's similar encounter with Hurstwood, Charles Norris's favorite character in fiction.

Despite the solider literary debts, most of the novel embraces the claptrap of the popular romance, complete with Zelda's rather hollow self-sacrifice that is more costly to her fiancé and her friends than to herself. Dr. Boylston's mundane but prescient observation to Zelda in chapter 1 (which itself ends on a melodramatic note) is a kind of thesis for the novel: "You might be a great actress someday, if you wanted to, but you'll have to learn how to feel first, and then learn how to express that feeling" (20).

Too often the language of the novel in its triteness is cloyingly appropriate to the theme. Zelda's "paroxysm of joyous excitement" (31) is straight out of a nineteenth-century pot boiler. Zelda's rejected lover, Gerry Page, sounds too often like a vengeful villain of melodrama: "You were free and easy before you married the ham actor; there's no reason why you can't be nice to me now" (287). Even Zelda's ideal man, the original playwright Tom Harney, lapses into clichés: " 'Zelda, Zelda!' he burst out, 'I cannot go on without you! You are the beginning and the end of everything for me; your smile, your laugh, your voice, are all I live for' " (389). It is almost as if Charles were mocking the very tradition that, through the heavy sales of Kathleen's works, was feeding them.

But then there is also much of his typically fine imagistic language that reveals the emotional nuances of his characters as

well as the specifics of his settings. Regarding the traumatic
night she climbed from her bedroom window and went to
Boylston's hotel, Zelda remembers "how the horses' hoofs had
slipped on the wet cobbles" (61). While visiting Michael in St.
Ignatius's, Zelda is struck by the "odorous" chemicals: "its smell
brought back a thousand nauseating memories: Boylston,
Boylston's office, the Emergency and the City and the County
hospitals in San Francisco, Ward 35!" (455). Equally unappealing to her are "tiny bubbles in the corners of [Gerry Page's]
mouth" (256) that become the refrain of his continued failure
to consummate their flirtation. Norris's description of a grog-
blossomed Selby shortly before his suicide shows succinctly
how much this once handsome man has deteriorated: "His face
had become bloated, fine crooked veins wriggled over his
cheeks, the whites of his eyes had grown blue and lumpy, the
eyes themselves bulged, a trifle glassy. . . . She shuddered at
the thought that she had once known him intimately" (437).

Norris continues his successful attempts to capture the
atmosphere of the 1890s. During her first stay in New York,
Zelda looks out the window of her tiny brownstone apartment
as she washes her only "silk waist" in the basin:

Beads of perspiration covered her forehead. And now and then little
trickles ran down between her breasts. A suffocating day, one of New
York's worst.
   Nevertheless, there was something exciting about the heat, Zelda
found; the hotter it grew the more exciting it became. . . . Windows
stood wide, revealing interiors of bedrooms in which figures in weird
scanty attire appeared and disappeared; some of these lolled across
stone sills to complain of the heat to acquaintances in other windows,
occasionally shrilling an irritable admonition to an indifferent offspring on the pavements below. Toward evening, groups began to
gather on stoops, the women in thin white dresses, the men coatless
and vestless, talk arose, a pleasant lightness in voices, laughter,
good-humored protests, the bass rumble of masculine chaffing, girlish
peals, the distant jingle of a hurdy-gurdy, a piano somewhere, singing,
children darting from curb to curb, their piping cries like needle stabs
in the dusk. (119)

Hungry and tired from making unsuccessful rounds of the
theatrical agents that same hot summer, Zelda must withstand

even the temptations of a candy store that she cannot afford: "A cool current blew upon her face from the shop's interior, . . . electric fans spun noiselessly bearing on the iced air the sweet odor of chemically flavored ice cream. Two girls at the marble counter of the soda fountain sucked straws plunged into the depths of tall, frosted glasses" (146–47). She lies awake at night listening to the various sounds of the city until "Those sounds gradually faded into silence, only the roar of the elevated at less and less frequent intervals, and the murmur of the city about her, like the subdued throbbing of a great heart. Often a long draught of cold water would stop the gnawing in her stomach, still it long enough for her to get to sleep" (157).

In his portrayal of Zelda's earlier frustrations, Norris moves candidly from her increasing boredom "with the dreary routine of her days" with Boylston to her unhappy attitude toward unwanted sex with Selby. While waiting for Boylston, "She would yawn, stretch, and languidly consider how the day should be spent. . . . She might contemplate taking a bath or doing some sewing. She did not bathe very often. The books she read were always novels of sticky romances or thrilling adventure" (99). And, regarding Selby, "she had minded dreadfully, his drinking himself into a maudlin, silly, staggering state . . . and disgusting her by love-making" (183). Zelda's compensatory love of her pet animals—"there was a loving fierceness in the clasp with which she suddenly hugged him [her dog, Buster] to her" (192)—is described with the same intensity used when she confesses her past sexual escapades to Tom Harney, a candid confession that also serves as another convenient summary for the reader: "The history of those years came slowly, each incident wrung from her. . . . She told of Michael, told of Boylston, and with shut eyes even told of the time when she had divided her favors between them . . . the miserable hand to mouth existence, Gerry, the sacrifice [abortion] of her child . . . her descent into the valley of the shadow" (392).

The weaknesses of the novel include the use of coincidence, particularly in Zelda's accidental meeting of Michael on an otherwise deserted beach. Zelda's childlike desire to leave Tom's successful play to "get back to first principles" (484) as Michael's nurse and cook (an act that looks forward in spirit to the conclusion of *Hands*) is not quite compatible with her joy in acting and her deep love and respect for Tom. More than most of Norris's novels, *Zelda Marsh* is in danger of becoming soap opera. Her marriage to fellow actor George Selby offers an interesting parallel to Carrie Meeber's relationships with both Drouet and Hurstwood but realizes no comparable depth of treatment. Her youthful affair with Michael has at times a poignant charm and renders her later decision to return to him plausible, if not convincing, but is without the warmth and trenchancy of Sam Smith's affair with Evelyn in *Pig Iron*.

Yet, while *Zelda Marsh* does not show an overall development of his art, Norris again presents the action freshly from a woman's point of view. He confronts such issues as abortion and double standards directly and honestly. Although the lukewarm reviews were deserved, the clarity and aptness of individual scenes remain in the memory. They testify to the judgment that he has written a novel not only "worth writing" but also worth reading.

Chapter Five
Seed and *Zest*

Seed: The Planting

Bart Carter, who is nine when *Seed* opens in 1890, slowly emerges as the central protagonist. He is the eighth of nine children of Captain Dan Carter, an aggressive Southerner who moved to California, eloped with Mathilda Crane, a staunch Catholic, built up a cattle and fruit ranch outside of Guadalupe, and founded the town of Carterville. During his parents' twenty-fifth wedding anniversary, Bart witnesses his father's overtures to cousin Philo's attractive and passionate Spanish wife, Anna. When his father is shot and killed in an ambush, Bart is convinced that Philo is the murderer but, without proof, must remain silent.

Book 2 opens in 1900 with Bart now working for his hated cousin Philo who, after Anna's death, took over management of the ranch at the request of Mathilda. When he is rejected by Philo's daughter, Jane, Bart seeks comfort with the lower-class Pudgie Cook, gets her pregnant, steals two hundred dollars from the ranch safe, and goes to San Francisco to begin his short-lived first marriage in a cheap rooming house. His brother Jack marries Jane. Pudgie dies after the birth of her stillborn child, closing one phase of Bart's life and opening another. By publishing his eyewitness account of the San Francisco earthquake in a New York paper, he is able to quit his job as a railroad clerk for a writing position on the *San Francisco Call.* There he has a passionate affair with a fellow journalist and poet, Norah Sue Crothers, contracts a venereal disease from her, and succumbs to depression and drink. With the help of two of his older brothers, Josh (a physician, now calling himself J. David Carter) and Francis (a Catholic priest), he begins his recovery and returns to writing.

Book 3 opens in 1910, when Bart at twenty-nine is recuperating at his boyhood ranch, Los Robles, now run by Jack and Jane. There he falls in love with Jane's younger sister, Peggy, marries her, and takes her to New York City, where he gets a job on a literary magazine (*Crosby's*) that had taken some of his stories. When the babies begin to arrive, Gill (Jack's twin brother, now a successful New York business-man) gets Bart a better paying job with a commercial maga-zine. In his spare hours Bart manages to write and publish a novel.

By the time book 4 opens in 1920, Peggy, afraid to have another child and refusing to practice birth control, has de-nied Bart her bed. The thirty-nine-year-old father of five chil-dren, burdened by household responsibilities and frustrated in his writing career and sex life, renews his friendship with a former fellow worker at *Crosby's,* Mildred Bransom, who of-fers him the literary encouragement and sexual satisfaction that Peggy is either unable or unwilling to offer. The rela-tionship becomes an affair. Peggy returns to Los Robles with the children where she remains, refusing to see a repentant Bart.

When book 5 opens it is 1930. Bart is now Bartholomew Carter, a successful popular novelist. He has been with Mildred for most of the intervening years, enduring her neurotic possessiveness along with her shrewd literary acumen and keen business sense. Finally gathering the courage to leave Mildred, Bart returns to the ranch where his brother, Father Francis, is dying. He and Peggy both promise him that they will reconcile the marriage. The novel ends with their passionate hope for a fresh start.

The Reviews

Seed, Norris's "Novel of Birth Control," got the extensive coverage one would expect of a book in 1930 about such a daring topic. That the majority of reviews were mixed or unfavorable was not, however, mainly the result of moral outrage or offended sensibilities. Despite the usual praise for his painstaking research and his dogged workmanship, most reviewers felt that he had written one of his weakest books. The *Saturday Review of Literature* for September 1930 provided a typical negative report:

Mr. Norris is a preacher with a numerous audience, but his latest fictionalized sermon is so ambiguous that his parishioners may not know what to make of it. His theme is birth control, and most of his characters are Catholics whose church forbids the practice. For several hundred pages he seems to be arguing that the Church is wrong; then he appears to hold that the Church is right; and finally he turns his story into an open forum, his characters spouting long speeches . . . that sound as if they were straight from the Catholic Encyclopedia and the standard works of Neo-Malthusian sociology.

The reviewer saw so "many characters . . . that the author himself cannot always keep track of them. . . ."[1] The *Nation,* on 27 August 1930, called *Seed* "more of a disquisition than a novel. . . . [Norris] supports his theme by a tedious citation of numerous horrible examples whose misery is ascribed to uncontrolled procreation." Grudgingly admitting that "as a competent analysis of passion, love and parenthood, this work is eminently satisfying," the reviewer concluded that "as a novel it remains lethargic and overlong."[2] Writing for the *Spectator,* on 20 December 1930, V. S. Pritchett voiced the British discontent with *Seed:* "unfortunately the author is not detached from [the hero]. The book contains a great host of characters and scenes and is not much more than an interesting accumulation."[3] And to the Reverend Joseph McSortey of the *Catholic World,* in October 1930, *Seed,* "though an interesting story, is not a weighty contribution to the literature of social betterment." His reasons soon become clear: "Our chief criticism of *Seed,* then, is that quite unconsciously the author leaves with the reader an incorrect, because inadequate, notion of the Catholic view on Birth Control."[4] Alan Reynolds Thompson (in the September 1930 issue of the *Bookman*) argued that "Norris is unable to transcend his thesis. . . . His title will win him many immature readers; but . . . with a pedestrian and humorless style, a rambling and unexciting plot, and carefully differentiated but charmless characters he offers too little. . . ."[5] Mary Ross, in a 17 August 1930 review for the *New York Herald Tribune Books,* attacked what she saw as "the smug and competent self assurance of the point of view [which] smothers . . . any chance the story afforded to create a living character."[6] Fanny Butcher of the *Chicago Daily Tribune,* on 23 August 1930, was somewhat kinder to the novel, allowing that "Norris has done something more than a case history" and "If *Seed* weren't so obviously propaganda ['a preachment against too prolific childbearing'] it would be an interesting picture of three generations of a buxom family drawn with meticulous care. . . ." To Butcher, "*Seed* is a novel of heroic proportions. . . . You know the characters when he finishes . . . and [*Seed*] would have heroic quality if it were not so concerned with proving something."[7]

Even the friendlier reviews were tempered with reservations. Horace Gregory of the *New York Evening Post,* on 16 August 1930, wanted to appreciate *Seed* more than he was able, and acknowledged that "Incidentally Mr. Norris gives us excellent pictures of life on a California ranch and a handful of rich details concerning the economic struggles of a writing man." Other positive aspects of *Seed* were obscured by Gregory's concern with the "Days of Zola and Muckrakers" that were "Recalled in New Work." He lamented that even Charles's predecessors "Theodore Dreiser and Upton Sinclair suffered most acutely from the congenital diseases transferred to them by the intrepid Zola; Frank Norris and Jack London slightly less so."[8] The *Springfield Sunday Union,* on 14 September 1930, worried that *Seed* would be unjustly "Bostonized" ("as was Mr. Dreiser's *American Tragedy*") and claimed that while "its plot is not one of the sort that gets one worked up" and

its situations are subjectively rather than objectively dramatic. . . . Its persons . . . are interesting to observe and compare with similar specimens in real life . . . one must admire the climactic planning and management which leads up to and makes the consideration of the question of birth control pertinent and appropriate. . . . The whole point of *Seed* is the desirability of the revision of our legislation such as will permit judicious and wholesale instruction on the subject—taking it out of the realm of the theological and clerical dogma and dealing with it from the viewpoint of economic, social and physical welfare.[9]

According to John Chamberlain in the *New York Times Book Review* for 17 August 1930, although "the author depends on too much environmental detail . . . the story has undoubted merits—its author's patience, knowledge of his California background and entire willingness to deal honestly and unflinchingly with a subject that Anthony Comstock liked to think of as strictly taboo. . . ." Chamberlain saw *Seed* as "a roman à thèse, but not offensively so, for there is no preaching in it that does not spring from the point of view of one character or another." He wished, however, that the "plausible" motivations had been rendered more consistently dramatically rather than "simply adumbrated," forcing "the reader . . . to be his own dramatist."[10]

Finally, Harry Hanson of the *New York World* argued that *Seed* "would have been more effective had it been biased one way or the other, and the suffering had been more sharply etched, as it is in Frank Norris's McTeague, or in Stephen Crane's Maggie." He concluded that

Seed has the power of holding the reader's interest, and possibly making him debate the subject also. . . . It is written with dignity and restraint; it is not a novel of suggestion, nor will the sniffers and the snoopers be able to make anything of it. It appeals deliberately to those who want to think about a subject that is much discussed but rarely gets into print. And it is definitely not a sex novel. I am sure that it will stimulate discussion and that the reader will get a good deal out of the book.[11]

The Harvest

With a cast of characters in *Seed* so large as to require a diagram for Bart's family alone, Norris both taxed his inventiveness and drew heavily from his own life and those of his family and friends. Bart is born the same year as Norris; at the novel's close in 1930 both character and author are forty-nine. Although Charles did not grow up on either a cattle or fruit ranch he, like Frank, spent time getting firsthand knowledge of ranch life. The "tales of knights, princes and doughty warriors"[12] that young Bart tells to his cousin Jane in Philo's hayloft are the same stories that Frank told to Charles when they were boys. Bart's responsibilities as art editor of the Dawson Publishing Company's the *Shoe Aegis* are very close to many of Charles's duties as "man-of-all-work" on the *American:* "While Bart's official title was 'art editor,' his duties had little to do with art and less to do with those of an editor" (272).

As did Kathleen, Bart writes a description of the 1906 earthquake for an Eastern paper. His hopes for a job with the

New York editor who bought his stories come to fruition as did
Charles's and Frank's. Bart and Peggy's apartment hunting in
New York City is again drawn from the experiences of both
Norris brothers. Following Charles's and Kathleen's experience
they manage to feed themselves breakfast and supper on a
"dollar a day" and occasionally treat themselves "at a French or
Italian restaurant [to a] . . . six course table d'hote with wine"
for "fifty cents" (237). Both couples move to Port Washington
and join the Yacht Club during the early years of their marriage.
Bart, as did Kathleen, sells stories to *Post, Century,* and *Harpers.*
Mildred's astute management of Bart's literary sales mirrors
Charles's managerial efforts for Kathleen and himself: "I've an
up-and-alive new firm that will give you an advance of five
thousand and pay you a fifteen percent royalty or you'll not put
pen to contract!" (333). Mildred gets Bart "twenty-five thousand dollars" for the film rights to his third novel *The Hacienda*
(338), just as Charles made a comparable deal that allowed
Hollywood to "picturize" *Brass,* his own third novel.
   Literary sources are also evident in *Seed.* Bart takes money
out of a safe so that he, like Hurstwood, can afford to run off
with a woman. After he has closed the safe he, too, realizes that
what he has done is irrevocable: "With the click of the falling
tumblers, his alertness returned. He gazed with widening eyes a
moment at the closed door" (164). Earlier Bart's observations
of nature red in tooth and claw recall young Frank Cowperwood's encounter with the lobster and the squid:

[Bart] watched a flock of screaming gulls fighting over the refuse of
some ship's galley. It represented a good picture of life, he thought
gloomily—men and women scrambling and battling among themselves over a mess of garbage; some got big pieces; some got nothing;
some were lucky; some weren't. That was all there was to existence.
   He went inside, found an obscure corner in the rear of the boat and
began to write a poem about the analogy. (105)

Charles's description of the Carters' twenty-fifth wedding
anniversary feast recalls banquets in *McTeague* and *The Octopus.*
Another sample of the Norris brothers' common use of ironic
juxtaposition appears in Charles's variation on a detail in the
wedding scene in *McTeague.* Frank's description of the incon-
gruously new soles of McTeague's shoes as he kneels beside

Trina during their wedding ceremony is transformed into Mathilda's observation of Jack and Gill during a Solemn Mass: "Before her were the two darling boys, with cherub faces and innocent eyes, looking pure and sanctified in their robes and lace bound on the altar steps on either side of the priest, while there, protruding from beneath their garments as they knelt, were their shoes— . . . all four of them!—foul with filth and fresh manure!" (60).

After Bart has placed his "earthquake anecdotes" on the front page of the *New York Times,* he is flattered by the same kind of "literary dilletantes" that Frank wrote of so disparagingly. These "would-be poets, self-elected critics and wiseacres, who mixed their own salads and talked indiscriminately of free love and art . . . patted him on the back, told him he was clever, even persuaded him to recite some of his early poetry—that formless verse born of his boyish soul! They listened with turned-up eyes and rapt faces, and declared it good. He believed Norah Sue Crothers [who offers him false flattery along with a dose of venereal disease]" (184).

The striking parallels that do homage to memorable scenes from his literary superiors do not wholly compensate for this novel's weaknesses. Although *Seed* is one of Charles's most ambitious novels, it is artistically too often one of his clumsiest; there are, for instance, far too many clichés. At a climactic moment Mildred breaks into the regulation "paroxysm of sobbing" (378). Earlier Bart declares to her: "My life's dull as dish water" (290). It is perhaps appropriate that a callow, nineteen-year-old Bart spouts bathetic clichés during his first courtship: " 'Yes, yes, marry me, or wait for me, Jane, until I can come home, and take you away. I . . . I . . . oh, well, you know! . . . you're the only person I care about in this world. You're everything to me. You're the sun and the moon. . . . You're my eyes and my fingers and my ears and my nose. . . . you're life to me. I want you. I can't live without you. You're the girl of my heart, the girl of my dreams . . .' " (119). But thirty years later he calls upon the same kind of rhetoric during the crucial reunion scene with Peggy: "Don't turn me down, don't send me away from all I prize in life. . . . Peggy, darling, do you love me still? Do you love old Bart who took you with him to New York, who did the best he could for you when the babies were coming so fast, who many a time got the meals and washed the dishes, swept and made the beds when you were sick . . ." (421).

Still, Bart the writer (as well as Norris, much of the time) remains very conscious of his artistry, his style, and grows to object to the "inartistic, cheap . . . worst kind of literary clap-trap . . ." (371). He objects to eliminating one of his characters the easy way by inventing an accident, but is trapped by the demands of the popular magazines: "To get rid of the objectionable person adequately, convincingly, would take from fifteen to twenty thousand words, but Bart knew he could not afford to write so many and still keep his story within serial length" (371). He follows Mildred's expedient editorial advice reluctantly: " 'You've established your market . . . editors, publishers, movie producers, the public, all expect a certain kind of story from you. Why spurn the hand that feeds you?' " (372).

Nor do bad writing and weak characterization overwhelm the novel as a whole. Much of Norris's description is realistic and effective enough. Bart's mother, "once a comely girl," after nine children and twenty-five years with Captain Carter "bulged in front and had grown so wide of hip that her walk was slow and ponderous. A thick cushion of fat lay between her shoulder blades at the nape of her neck, and flabby bags of flesh swung to and fro from the underside of her fat arms. Across her high, smooth forehead, she wore a 'false front,' a band of tight brown curls, which she fastened to her real hair with invisible hairpins" (21). Charles juxtaposes the deliberately sentimental scene of Tilly's and Camilla's late-night confessions of their adolescent crushes with a description of their nine-year-old-brother Bart's inability to sleep because of a "deep choking emotion he could not name." His insomnia is prompted by the frightening encounter between his father and Anna that he had unwittingly observed (49–54). Charles's detailed description of the "bare ugly hotel room" where Bart and Pudgie spend their wedding night is only partially undercut by the overblown recollection of his fear of discovery. Bart recalls

the shuffling darkey in a frayed and spotted braided coat. He saw again the lumpy double bed with its darned and dingy spread, the limp lace curtains, the washbasin that showed discolored streaks where the drip fell from tarnished faucets, the varnished yellow dresser, the square table with its stiffly-starched scarf, the ribbed white porcelain match safe in its center, the black cloth-bound Bible! All night long, mixed with his graver fears, had been the additional one that from this cheerless refuge he and Pudgie might summarily be ejected should their unholy relationship be discovered!

(178–79)

Norris's three-and-a-half-page summary of the bittersweet months with Pudgie leading to her death in childbirth is convincingly done (178–81). So is his spare description of Bart's determination after his affair with Norah and his recovery at the ranch (186–88). A typical Sunday in Port Washington (269–71) for the seven Carters and Bart's typical day of "dull, deadly uninteresting work" at the *Shoe Aegis* office (272–75) are both masterly. Norris's dramatic presentation of Bart's stunned state shortly after the final rejection of his novel, *Quicksilver,* is equally effective:

He remembered standing in the Pennsylvania Station, his rejected manuscript under his arm, waiting for Peggy, who had brought the children to be photographed. . . . When she finally appeared, herding two boys before her, the toddling Janey's hand in hers, the two-months-old Margaret in her free arm, he saw she was on the point of collapsing with fatigue. He had not the heart to break the news to her then. As they stood waiting for the train gate to open, Janey's milk bottle, wrapped up along with the baby in her mother's arms, in some way slipped from the folds of the shawl and crashed to the stone pavement, splattering glass and milk for yards around. There had been a titter in the crowd. (268)

Norris also captures the then fashionable artsy decor of the studio apartment that Mildred has decorated. There is the "tall wide window of prismed glass," and "thin gold gauze curtains" for the daylight, with "thick folds of turquoise-blue velvet" for night, "a balcony . . . with a rather precipitous staircase leading from it to the studio floor and on the side opposite the great window . . . a hooded fireplace of noble proportions which projected ten feet into the room," a "large oil by Matisse, smaller canvases of Cézanne, Picasso and other moderns . . . an Italian altar cloth of matchless gold needlework surrounded by a dark plush crimson border" covering "the bare paneling of the

fourth wall . . . a black ebony piano . . . leather and uphol-
stered chairs of Italian design and workmanship, a carved chest,
massive gilded cathedral candlesticks, a broad flat-topped desk
. . . an escritoire a century in age, and book shelves—shelves
high and low, laden with books, crammed with books, overflow-
ing with books" (360). Bart reveals his growing disenchantment
with Mildred herself in his objective description of her: "Coldly
he regarded her as she continued to rage. An ugly woman,
when she was angry. . . . Her face was blotched, her bad eye
twitched and closed spasmodically, the tendons on her thin
neck stood out like whipcords" (369). Later, even when both
are in better moods, he sees her just as clearly: "In the strong
light of the north window he could . . . see the thick enamel of
make-up which coated her face. Mildred was thin. She had
dieted when he first knew her; now there was no occasion for it;
the past year or two had left her emaciated. In the garish
window light, her haggard, creamed and powdered face, with its
one sunken, discolored eye and richly carmined lips, looked
like a death's head" (374).

Norris gives Bart his own work habits along with his descriptive talents. When Bart is writing well, his "moments of
exaltation . . . made him get up early in the mornings and
whipped him on with ink-stained fingers late into the night.
When it deserted him, there was only grim determination left
to drive him on, forcing him to make his pen travel from line to
line, laboriously filling page after page" (275).

It is curious that Norris's only novel about a writer is also one
of his weakest. For *Seed* is not only more slow moving than his
previous novels, but at times does achieve the dullness that
Henry James found unpardonable in a novel. The discussions of
birth control are often as empassioned as those concerning
marriage in *Brass,* but not as effectively orchestrated, not as
carefully woven into the whole fabric of the book. There is a
disconcerting shrillness, for instance, in Josh's diatribes in favor
of birth control and sterilization.

Norris is, however, again in firm control of the analogical
details of structure, for although some of the minor characters
seem to get lost for a time, each character in some way
elucidates this issue of birth control that was more controversial
during the first two decades of the century than the issue of

abortion is today. His intention was not to write propaganda but to make people think. One of his points is that there are no clear-cut solutions to such complex issues. No matter what, life continues and certain things do not change very much. Just as Bart comes full circle back to the ranch of his birth, so his son moves easily into set patterns: "Dan slid . . . beneath the steering wheel, banged the door, and the car moved off . . . to the old barn. Bart remembered Josh performing the same service [forty years before],—driving his uncle's [horse and buggy] to cover" (416). While *Seed* is often not up to Charles's highest standards, it is another respectable effort worth reading. Most readers would be "very glad to have an inscribed copy" as, according to his own declaration, was Dreiser.[13]

Zest: The Plot

Zest traces the life of Robert Gillespie from his first ill-fated romance during his college days to his suicide at thirty-six after his jealous mistress fires a shot that paralyzes him.

Mrs. Robert Gillespie, Robert's mother, successfully discourages Robert's love affair with the socially unacceptable Dixey Nugent, and is matchmaker for her son's marriage to Penelope Vaughan, the aristocratic niece of the wealthy Mrs. Selby Covington. Having extracted himself from an unpleasant sexual relationship with Sally Wurtz, an office girl, Robert allows himself to be caught up in prenuptial activities that lead inexorably to his marriage. Penelope's playboy brother, Warner, marries Julia Loeb, daughter of wealthy but unpretentious parents whose company Robert appreciates more than Penelope does. The Gillespie marriage suffers from the absence of wealth and sexual compatibility. Penelope nearly dies from the birth of a baby she did not want. Afterward she first refuses Robert sex and eventually asks him for a divorce so she can marry Mr. Yerrington, a wealthy older man. Penelope takes with her Barbara, the child Robert has grown to love. Earlier Robert had had his own dalliance with Mrs. Vogel, a passionate older woman who offered him the sexual gratification that Penelope had refused. He accepted her financial assistance but, before any sexual consummation, ashamed and guilty, he broke off their relationship.

Book 2 opens with the diary entries of Captain Robert Gillespie from Camp Dix, New Jersey, during World War I. Divorced from Penelope, Robert falls in love with Bella Avery, his company commander's wife. They have a passionate affair which is curtailed by the objections of Bella's sister, the end of the war, and the illness and death of Robert's mother. Back in San Francisco, Robert courts and marries Julia Loeb (now widowed) and settles down to five years of success in business and in a marriage that has mutual friendship if not sexual passion.

In book 3 Bella arrives in San Francisco while Julia is away helping her prodigal brother. Renewal of their torrid affair prompts Robert to take an apartment with Bella and leave Julia. Barbara's arrival (after Yerrington's desertion has prompted Penelope's suicide) arouses jealousy in Bella, who has grown fat and lazy. Angered by Robert's threats to leave her, she shoots him, severing his spinal cord. After he has made sure that Barbara will be cared for, he commits suicide rather than face a life of continued paralysis.

Reviews

Zest gathered more grudgingly positive reviews than negative ones. George Dangerfield opened his *Saturday Review of Literature* piece, on 20 May 1933, declaring that he "cannot pretend to admire Mr. Norris as a novelist; he belongs to . . . the tractarian school of fiction. . . . But I am beginning to admire him as a minor prophet." He lamented, however, that Norris, unlike the older prophets, "does not" offer "at least a moral solution for living. . . ." Although "Mr. Norris is no mean artisan, and 'Zest' is well constructed . . . there is a poverty in it, a lack of poetry . . . it does not contain human beings but the data for human beings":

In another sense, however, its author's careful presentation—like his hard, unlovely prose—is oddly persuasive. . . . Women may not like it; but any man who has suffered . . . certain spiritual wounds at the hands of a woman will not fail to discover . . . something which answers to his own experience. . . . Mr. Norris has achieved something which is beyond the power of all but quite a few writers.[14]

While the *Times Literary Supplement,* on 29 August 1933, "found it hard to be even sorry for Robert Gillespie,"[15] Mary Ross, in her 21 May, 1933 review for the *New York Herald Tribune Books,* saw

Mr. Norris's portrait of Bob . . . not that of a gay Lothario, but of a man, genuinely pained by conflicting desires which he himself could not harmonize. . . .

The two spots of serenity in the book are in the old fashioned home of the Loebs, held together by the wisdom and devotion of the mother and Bob's decision to die. But the first was not enough to protect from disaster the children who grew up in that home; the latter brought integrity only for destruction.[16]

The *New York Times Book Review* of 21 May 1933 called Bob "a quite negligible figure" and *Zest* "unimportant as a social study or a work of creative literature," but added, "Yet there is a quality about all the novels of Charles G. Norris which raises him above the level of popular magazine fiction. That is a kind of dogged honesty, a refusal to play up to easily aroused and superficial emotions. . . . There is no touch of melodrama, false pathos, sentimentality or machine-made eroticism. . . . the novel is sound and workmanlike."[17]

The one-paragraph review in *Commonweal* for 11 August 1933 was one-sided, calling Norris, with no intent at flattering, "a lesser Dreiser." Although, according to *Commonweal,* "his prose is less bad" and "his novels are shorter . . . , the passages which move his characters are less moving to the reader. . . . Mr. Norris gives us the four-hundred and forty-five page story of . . . a man in no way extraordinary except for his dullness. . . . No pattern is imposed on the Zolaesque mess from which it is made; no skillful delineation justifies the use of clods for characters; not the faintest music stirs the leaden prose."[18]

After an inauspicious opening (that also invokes the spirit of Zola) the *Canadian Forum* for September 1933 was somewhat kinder to Norris's eighth novel: "This book, which might well bear the subtitle, 'Love-Life of a Lusty Lout,' is strongly recommended to anyone that wants a good deep revel in gloom. . . . The book is hard reading . . . yet its very drabness carries with it a heavier condemnation of our civilization . . . than more emphatic and rhetorical propaganda could achieve." It concluded that although *Zest* is "not a particularly memorable book" from "the literary point of view . . . as a document of social unrest among the supposedly privileged classes its value is far from negligible."[19]

The Making

Many of the autobiographical parallels in *Zest* recall Charles's memories of his father, his brother, Frank, and, of course, his mother, but more than in any of his other novels he drew upon his own army experiences. There are passages in *Zest* almost identical to those in his 1917–18 letters to Kathleen from Camp Dix.

Except for the slightly receding chin and hair color, the twenty-four-year-old Robert resembles Frank Norris at Berkeley in his early twenties. Charles playfully names Mrs. Gillespie's Japanese butler/cook, Frank. He has the wealthy Major Covington die the same year as Frank, 1902. And it is almost a précis of Gertrude Doggett Norris's version of her thwarted stage career and subsequent desertion, divorce, and settlement that Charles translated into Mrs. Gillespie's own truncated operatic career and marital complaints: "Bob's father had definitely promised he would in no way interfere with her professional career, but no sooner were they man and wife than he had opposed this in every way possible, triumphing at last when nature abetted him and she became pregnant. Two babies died in succession, and then Robert; and when the boy was ten years old Gillespie senior had begged for a divorce. Five hundred a month alimony had been managed, and upon this Bob's mother and he had lived during his highschool and college days."[20] Mrs. Gillespie's concert notices "all mentioned her stateliness and fine looks" (19), the precise phrase used to describe Gertrude even in her last years.

Penelope's difficult pregnancy, her confinement to bed and her "constant nausea," any "food too often [making] her ill" (118), is another replica of Kathleen's troubled pregnancy. Robert's and Penelope's sexual problems may also reflect Charles's and Kathleen's alleged sexual temperance after the deaths of their twin girls. Years after Barbara's birth Robert "could not remember just how long it had been since [Penelope] had given herself to him . . ." (190). His sex life with Julia years later is not much of an improvement: "It had been weeks now since anything had happened between them" (343).

An army career that is almost identical to Norris's provides Robert some compensation for his inadequate sex life. His professional duties including those as "Officer in Charge of Firing" (212) are largely Norris's own. The diary entries that open book 2 detail such activities so familiar to Norris as his training of troops and drawing up the schedule of firing. Norris and Robert both receive promotions to captain and then major. They also share a fervent desire for active combat and, frustrated, leave the army with the feeling that "the war had passed [them] by" (270). Earlier Robert echoes Norris's exact sentiments: "This war may hold disappointment for me, but none will be any keener than the sight of my boys marching off in the snow at ten o'clock at night with their packs and their rifles on their shoulders, and—without their captain" (211–12).

One of Norris's social comforts during his assignment at Camp Dix was the close proximity of Kathleen, Teresa, and the children in Mount Holly. Bella and her sister arrange for similar housing: "The first of April saw the three girls, with much hilarity, and excitement, take possession of . . . a large square brick farmhouse, a mile and a half outside of Mount Holly" (232). One of Norris's grimmest experiences was the 1918 flu epidemic which killed thousands, including Teresa. In *Zest* "the influenza struck Dix . . . like a devastating wind. No poison gas could have done its work better." Bella hysterically reports that her sister Nelly, "taken ill on Monday . . . was dead" (276). At the war's end Charles and Kathleen traveled back to San Francisco, he to show Gertrude his uniform, she for an operation. After his release from the army Robert returns in uniform to San Francisco for his mother's surgery.

Robert's postwar weekends and vacations with Julia and the Loeb family at their ranch, which provide some of his happiest times, are drawn from the Norris family's own experiences at their Saratoga ranch, their summer paradise that by 1933 offered Charles over a dozen years of memories. Charles's almost obsessive concern for cleanliness at both his formal Palo

Alto home and the Saratoga ranch, where he personally checked picture frames and doortops for dust, shows up on Captain Gillespie's "white cotton glove" test for "evidence of grease" in the army kitchen (243). Always at the Loeb house they enjoy the same games the Norrises played with their children and guests: " 'Buzz,' 'Jenkins,' 'You Have a Face' and 'The Prince of Paris Lost His Hat' " (73). Even the "swell popovers" the Loebs relish for breakfast again recall those Kathleen would serve at the ranch by tossing them across the table.

Traces of *Zest*'s literary sources, however, are not as readily apparent as in many of Charles Norris's other novels. Even Frank's influence is harder to find, although it is apparent in Robert's expressed desire to have "a girl who's your chum" (210), a desire Condy Rivers comes to feel in *Blix,* and in Robert's guilty feelings about Sadie Wurtz who "appealed to the animal side of him of which he was ashamed" (53), feelings that Vandover harbors regarding his seduction of Ida Wade. There may be a less rhythmical echo of Dickens's classic fog-enveloped opening of *Bleak House* (first read to Charles by Gertrude) in the description of an August dog day at Camp Dix:

Dust lay in thick layers upon the roads, in soft powdery ridges along their sides, silvering the stalks of withered grass that had died there; it coated thresholds, porches, sills, drifted in through open windows and left its gritty touch in beds, blankets, equipment, and rose in puffing, suffocating clouds to the tramp of feet. Leather-hued, somber, ugly, the great cantonment quivered beneath the merciless downpour. Only one note of color broke the drab monotony: the flag with its red stripes and blue field hanging limply from the peak of its tall flagstaff near Camp Headquarters. (265)

The Art and Message

In *Zest* there is also the usual mixture of bad writing and clichés with carefully crafted, dramatically effective prose. The dialogue at times goes beyond what is a legitimate attempt to capture the ineptness of character, as in Robert's "Gee, Miss Wurtz, let's you and I be friends" (15). "Gee" and "Gee whilikers" occur too frequently in his vocabulary. He often gives vent to his feelings in language that tends to be too extravagant, even for a callow youth. The mutual admiration exchanged between Robert and Julia during their early lunches is also excessive; so are Robert's expansive feelings for his golf partners when he is more mature: "Bob glanced at the faces of his companions, and his heart grew big with affection. They were his true best friends, and wonderfully fine men, all of them . . . big men, strong men, men with brains and force. A man was rich indeed with such fellows as close friends" (358). Charles's foreshadowing also can be heavy-handed. After Robert dines "in happy accord" the night of Penelope's return from New York, the omniscient narrator remarks: "It was the last time they were to be so" (154). Even Charles's repetition of the quotation from Isaiah 4:1 ("And in that day seven women shall take hold of one man") lacks the impact of his similar use of biblical refrain in *Salt,* which had so moved F. Scott Fitzgerald.

The more effective touches include the sunny day in San Francisco which opens *Zest,* offering a false note of hope whose irony becomes apparent in an increasingly gloomy book. When his colors are bright Charles is usually pointing up unpleasantness and often foreboding, as in an early scene with Robert and Penelope after a fashionable dance:

The hall light in the blistered colored globe on top of the newel post was burning as he opened the Vaughans' door with Penelope's latchkey. Blots of blue, red, and green lay in fantastic circles on walls and floors. Sprawled upon the lower steps lay the figure of Warner Vaughan, his soiled hat at his feet, his hair a disorderly shock over his eyes. His unbuttoned overcoat disclosed his rumpled shirt front, his sagging wilted collar, and the dangling strings of his bow tie. (32)

Robert's "sordid experience" with Sadie Wurtz, although not as colorful, is to the point:

the cheap room, the cheap towel, the bed, the mean, ugly furniture, the banging, loud laughing and rough voices which echoed continuously through the place, undeadened by the thin walls.

After Sadie had departed, he bathed in a cracked enamel tub, dressed, and walked dismally homeward, feeling dirty in body and mind, despising himself. (51)

His reactions are very much those that Penelope will feel after each of his rare sexual encounters with her. Robert's unconsummated amorous relationship with his wealthy client is an analogy to his liaison with Bella Avery. Norris introduces it with abrupt simplicity: "Bob had an odd experience while Penelope was away. A divorced lady by the name of Mrs. Vogel fell in love with him" (168). Later in the novel, sated by an afternoon of passion with Bella, Robert's interest in sleeping with her that night recalls his aversion to Mrs. Vogel's pleas "for one night in each other's arms" (170). Robert "looked down into [Bella's] shining eyes. His own were vague. After the afternoon experience, the prospect of what she was suggesting did not appeal to him as being particularly tempting" (252). The shallowness of his liaison with Bella is neatly revealed in a scene in which she is so anxious to tell him of her past affairs that she fails to hear his own attempts to do the same.

Typically effective with details about such things as army paper work, Norris is also effective in his descriptions and his structural use of dreams. He foreshadows Robert's own peccadilloes in his dream of his mother standing at "the edge of a cliff" and "pointing to the sea and telling him something shocking about his father" (127). Later Robert dreams that while he is embracing Julia she turns into Bella's dead sister, Nelly: "it was her corpse that he held in his arms!" (301). The dream signals the failure of his marriage to Julia, his affair with Bella, and his own sudden death. Wide awake, he also registers fleeting glimpses that serve as minor epiphanies, as when he sees Julia's n'er-do-well brother "driving a blonde girl up Market Street in a shabby motor car" (394), again prefiguring his own sordid affair with Bella. The glib advice of Robert's bachelor friend, Jim Cameron, offers sophistic support for Robert's renewed affair with Bella; Cameron convinces Robert that it is natural to love more than one woman. The assurance paves the way for Robert's rationalizations and his affair (373).

Although *Zest* is another of Charles Norris's novels with too much melodrama and too many coincidences, it is in the main a realistic picture of a weak-willed man too much under the influence of a domineering mother, a man who ultimately has no zest for life and is unable to cope with the multifarious pressures of life. Norris achieves moments of power and some

perceptive insights into the son who seems doomed to repeat
his father's actions, the actions of a man he scarcely knew. Bella
Avery also emerges as a finely conceived, complex creation.
Even though *Zest* is not as consistently good as *Salt, Brass,* or
Pig Iron, Norris's hand is more often sure than not. While
Robert's suicide is a bit abrupt, it is prepared for and appropriate, as a happy ending would not have been. It is a step beyond
the stagey call of S.O.S. at the end of *Pig Iron.* Nor does Norris
wax didactic with the quotation from *Isaiah.* He leaves the
reader to draw his own conclusions regarding the impact of
"seven women" taking "hold of one man."

Chapter Six
Hands, Bricks without Straw, and Flint

Hands: The Plot and the Reception

Charles Norris's ninth novel, *Hands,* focuses on three generations of the Baker family of California in three books, entitled
"Michael," "Martin," and "Miles." Michael, son of Jonathan, a
failed prospector, is happy with his carpenter's profession but
unhappy with his wife, Carrie, who, after bearing three children
in rapid succession, remains sexually unappealing. In love with
Kate Maloney, the maid of his boss (B. F. Walker), he becomes
bitterly jealous of his handsome younger brother, Luke, who
marries her. After unsuccessful attempts to break up their
marriage, he seduces Luke's new wife. Kate dies after the birth
of Michael's daughter. Michael joins B. F. Walker's church in a
state of partial repentance, only to die of a heart attack when
years later he learns that his son, Martin, has unwittingly
married his own half sister.

Martin leaves San Francisco for the Klondike, where he
works hard and brings back a small fortune. His first marriage is
annulled. After being rejected by Gertie Trimble, his sister
Ida's roommate, he marries B. F. Walker's daughter, Mary; he
survives the 1906 San Francisco earthquake to amass a fortune
in the construction business, and invests in the stock market.
His wife remains fonder of her social whirl than of him.
Divorced from the invigorating manual labor of his youth,
feeling rejected by his family, a middle-aged Martin shoots
himself after losing his money in the 1929 stock market crash.

Miles goes reluctantly from college to the Columbia University School of Architecture at his father Martin's insistence and
expense. He cares more for dances and parties than school, and
he dates socialite Dorothy Knox until he falls in love with Nora
Shaughnessy, a struggling actress. She refuses to marry him and

leaves New York to have their son in secret. Martin's bankruptcy forces Miles to seek manual labor. Back in California he
meets and marries Nora and, like his grandfather years before,
delights in building their house with his own hands.

While reviewers saw in *Hands* some of the same defects they
had seen in *Zest* and in most of Norris's previous novels, they
tended to be kinder toward his treatment of at least two of the
three generations in *Hands* than they were toward *Zest*'s darker
biography of Robert Gillespie.

Positive reviews of John O'Hara's *Butterfield 8* and *Hands*
shared the same page of the 19 October 1935 *Saturday Review
of Literature*. Max Miller admired how "Mr. Norris constructs
brick by brick, soul by soul, the affairs of a family which in 1880
started as carpenters and by 1935 had swung full circle . . .
back to the same occupation. . . . [He] is at home in the San
Francisco of forty years ago as well as today, and his scenes are
splendid with accuracy." Miller especially praised "the first
book," which "is likely to remain registered in one's mind long
after the subsequent two." Although he objected to Norris's
not "proving anything new" or "pointing towards any solution,"
he praised his "skill as a writer to make everything seem
fresh. . . ."[1] The *Christian Science Monitor* for 22 October 1935
summarized what it took to be the novel's "theory," that "the
springs of happiness lie in the individual, that a willing worker
can gain security no matter where he is," and called *Hands* "a
long but continuously interesting novel, possibly one of the
finest Mr. Norris has done."[2] Stanley Young of the *New York
Times Book Review* of 20 October 1935 called *Hands* "his finest
work. . . . Mr. Norris has a strenuous mind. He can see
American life with the honesty and reality of a Wharton or a
Glasgow when he forgets to labor a theme, and he can build up
characters who move under a powerful emotional impetus. . . .
he seems [in *Hands*] to be moving unconsciously . . . to free
himself from the iron heel imposed by a thesis. For the purpose
of his considerable art, this move is of major importance."[3]

The *Chicago Tribune* for 25 October 1935 thought the novel
too long and the third section "dead on the vine," but concluded that on the basis of two thirds of the writing, while *Hands*
was not "Mr. Norris's best novel it is a pretty good novel. . . ."[4]
Contrarily, the *New Statesman and Nation*, on 25 January 1936,

declared *Hands* "not a good novel" but, nevertheless, "painstaking and thorough," containing "an extremely interesting picture of social change at a period when the America that collapsed in the depression was just coming into existence."[5] The *Boston Evening Transcript,* on 2 November 1935, was more favorable: "Mr. Norris tells . . . things in a rather coarse, heavy and often melodramatic style, that suits the dark color of his character. He shapes the material with so much conviction in his own mind the reader comes near to believing in the hackneyed climax in . . . 'Michael.' . . . The Klondike, the World's Fair, the World War, the stock market crash are all imbedded here in substantial settings. Over a wide canvas roam a furiously writhing ant-heap of manifold characters, all adequately, at times poignantly created. . . ."[6] And even to the somewhat less enthusiastic *Springfield Sunday Union and Republican,* in December 1935, *Hands* "is an absorbing, if not wholly coherent tale" in which "the author writes earnestly and tensely of everything he would describe whether it be an earthquake or the luxurious fittings of Martin's home."[7]

Herschel Brickell in the 7 December 1935 *New York Post* labeled *Hands* "a solid chronicle of the shifting American scene,"[8] but Mary Ross of the *New York Herald Tribune Books,* on 20 October 1935, was again neither so succinct nor so favorable. Ross "can see no way to read this story except that a harsh and narrow life complicated the inner conflicts of those who sweated and corrupted that scene no less than did the luxury of the children's children. . . ." She argued further that the book's exhortation that work is "our salvation. Toil! That will set us on the right road again," is contradicted by the lives of Norris's characters and far too simplistic a solution. She concluded: "Forceful because of the closeness and of its questions and Mr. Norris's skill as a story teller, *Hands* vividly reflects the current confusion as to the values of the American past and present and of individual lives and the setting which molds them and is in turn molded by them."[9] Mary Ross was a long-time skeptic of Charles Norris's work. Yet in her confusion over his alleged attempts to reflect in this novel "the current confusion" about American values she was not alone among the reviewers. Norris succeeded in his attempt to make them think; he failed, however, to help them to think clearly.

Sources

As in most of Norris's work, it is hard here to avoid autobiographical materials. B. F. Walker, for instance, takes considerably more than his first two initials from B. F. Norris. He also builds cheap houses in San Francisco (as does Vandover's father in Frank Norris's *Vandover and the Brute*). Also like the senior Norris, B. F. is "a leading elder" and teaches Sunday school in the Presbyterian church and greatly admires Dwight D. Moody. Nor would B. F. Walker's motto be anathema to B. F. Norris: "Believe in God and it's money in your pocket. . . ."[10] Like Gertrude Doggett Norris, Nora Shaughnessey's mother is an ex-actress who "loved her Shakespeare and Browning," and urges her child to excel in the arts. And in the spirit of B. F. Norris, Miles says to Nora " 'there's nothing in this stage business for you. You and I gotta get married' " (437).

Probably still haunted by the traumatic effect on the family of Lester's sudden death, Charles has Martin's handsome younger brother, Johnny, also die of diphtheria. Martin, like Frank, engages in soldiering abroad where he, also like Frank, acquires typhoid and is "invalided home" (138). Earlier Martin breaks his arm (as Frank did in his teens) and he, too, avoids formal education at a crucial time in his life as it becomes "too late" for his father "to try to get him into any school" (312–14). Nor had Charles forgotten the nature of Frank's own sudden death. Laura Trimble dies of "A burst appendix, peritonitis" (278–79).

There do not seem to be as many obvious literary borrowings in *Hands* as in most of the previous novels. (One early exception could be the children's street fight in chapter 1, which is similar to the opening battle of the urchins in Stephen Crane's *Maggie*). Traces of Frank Norris's influence are perhaps found in the physical descriptions of the two women most important to Martin. Gertie Trimble is another big woman like some of his own heroines and many of his brother's. Martin is tempted to do with her what Ross Wilbur actually does with the Viking heroine of *Moran of the Lady Letty:* "If she were a man, he would like to wrestle with her, grapple with her, throw her. It would be exciting to get a head lock on her, feel her arms roughly clasp his waist, as she strained and struggled in his grip" (213).

The jumbled snatches of conversation at the Martin Baker's bridge party, the mingling of social gossip and talk of stock market deals recall the opening scene in *The Pit*. The advice Martin's wealthy partner gives to Miles (which is unhappily ignored by both Miles and Martin) is the same sound advice ignored by Curtis Jadwin of *The Pit* before his bankruptcy: " 'I tell you boy, you leave the stock market alone. It will skin you alive; take your shirt' " (409).

Assessment

Hands suffers from Norris's usual lapses in technique. The coincidence of Mrs. Vance entering the room at the precise time of Martin's and Mary's first kiss is stagey, and certain of his parallels are forced, as in Mrs. Walker's admonition of Mary: " 'Don't acknowledge that boy's bow, Mary. He's only a carpenter's son.' " As she sweeps by, the omniscient narrator adds that she entered "the church for the services commemorating the birth of another carpenter's son born nearly two thousand years before" (136). Some of the descriptions are pathetically overdone: " 'Oh's and ah's' of suffering, notes of agony were torn from [Miles] as he kissed [Nora] and at length his head went down upon her furry shoulder with an escaping groan" (417). Although Nora is wearing a fur coat, the scene (reminiscent of Fitzgerald's objections to Norris's description of Philip Baldwin's rather apelike morning ritual in *Brass*) seems more appropriate to a cage in the Bronx Zoo than the front seat of Miles Baker's sports car. At times Miles's actions in Nora's absence are equally atavistic: "At night he bit his wrists, shut fast his eyes and longed for her" (441). And when she returns from a theatrical tour his actions are rather overexuberantly described: "Miles leaped upon his own bed, buried his face in his pillow, wriggled in ecstasy, kicking his legs" (456).

Still, the stronger passages once again offset most of the distracting stylistic infelicities. Norris's opening panoramic description of San Francisco as it must have been in 1880, seen from the roof of a house on the crest of one of the city's "steepest hills," is excellent, as is the description of the claustrophobic bathroom that is Michael Baker's pride (19). Norris, more importantly, captures with psychological realism

Carrie's abrupt but perceptive accusation made to an unsuspecting Michael as they lie together in bed: "You're jealous of Luke 'cause everybody likes him. Y'u pretend y'u care about his drinkin'. Y'u don't do nothin' of the kind; y'u egg him on to git drunk. Oh, I know. You're hopin' some day he'll fall down and break his neck, or somebody in a fight will hurt him real bad. An' all the time you're pretendin' to Kate you're sech a good friend of his'n and you're trying to keep him from goin' bad ways!" (82). That Michael thought his actions had gone undetected underlines the extremity of his destructive self-absorption. Norris also captures well the details of D. W. Moody's revivalist meeting (93–100); Michael is an unforgettable convert poring "over the pages of the Bible, underscoring passages and writing comments on the margins of the leaves the way he knew Sturgis, B. F. and Moody did" (107).

The switch from the blunted awareness of Michael to the more acute center of consciousness of Martin is smoothly handled. Michael's physical consummation of his insidious passion for Kate neatly parallels Martin's equally ominous consummation of his innocent love for his half sister, the illicit offspring of his father's union. The brisk dialogue between Martin and Gertie is compensation for the absence of any mutual sexual interest. Norris also shows in *Hands* that he could set a scene with graceful prose: "It was a warm June Sunday morning, the windows had been opened wide and the limp net curtains sucked against the screening and ballooned away from it as the draft came and went through the open door" (258). The graphic description of Miles's painful early encounter with manual labor aptly prepares for the pleasures of his later successes that take the thematic action full circle to the opening biblical quotation from Ephesians 4:28:

Let him who stole steal no more: but rather let him labour, working with his hands the thing which is good, that he may have to give to him that needeth.

Even though Mary Ross is too literal-minded in her demand that Norris resolve the contradictions in his novel, contradictions that few wholly resolve in their lives, Norris's use of the biblical quotation is a bit muddy; so is the purpose of such analogical details as the reference in book 2 (264) to the college professor's cottage foreshadowing Miles's own cottage, which, of course, parallels the house that grandfather Michael Baker built with his own hands. For what is the reader to make of these parallels? Certainly the college professor had little to do with the building of his cottage, and Michael's joy in his carpentry does not offset his dissatisfaction with his life.

Perhaps one of the strongest aspects of *Hands,* however, lies in the structural parallels in the three books that do work. Each of the three men is indifferent to or distrustful of his father. Each is adversely affected by love affairs with women. At the same time they seem such different men. Norris controls the often ironic nuances of their differences and similarities masterfully. The weakest (Miles) is promised the most happiness. The book focusing on Miles, however, is decidedly less interesting than the books featuring Michael and Martin. Book 3 is also anticlimactic. Yet it comes alive when Norris deals with the impact of the stock market crash on the idle rich. The writing here is as good as his discussion of the earthquake and its economic impact in book 2. Miles is less interesting than his jealous grandfather. The self-made Martin, totally bankrupt by the crash and emotional isolation, is more interesting than his self-indulgent son. The reader is genuinely moved by Martin's suicide in book 3 because he has learned to care for him in book 2.

Hands in book 3 seems to be in the mainstream of novels dealing with the alleged purity of America's agrarian past, but the happy pastoral ending, however well intentioned, is forced and contrived. Even if the reader were to accept Miles's transformation, the seeds of the change have not been planted soon enough to produce a hearty plant. It is mostly because of the flaws in this last book that *Hands,* although one of his most ambitious and most promising efforts, is not one of Charles Norris's most successful novels.

Bricks without Straw: Plot and Reviews

Bricks without Straw deals with two generations of conformity and rebellion in the Kennedy family. Jerry Kennedy leaves the Midwestern town of St. Cloud in 1904. Having graduated from St. Cloud University, he seeks escape in New York City from the restrictive conservative influence of his father, a wealthy banker and prominent church elder. He finds a beautiful free-spirited singer, Connie Consuello, falls in love with her, gets her pregnant, and marries her. She has a miscarriage. Financial reverses prompt them to return to his father's home, and he begins work in his father's bank. Stifled, Connie leaves within a year, aiding the elopement of Jerry's younger sister, Dorothea, who marries against Mr. Kennedy's wishes.

The second half of the book opens in 1931. Jerry has remained in St. Cloud and married the minister's daughter, Marianne, and has become a prominent banker and the president of the Country Club. He has adopted both Dennis, the son of the now deceased Connie and her second husband, and Jan, the daughter of Jerry's sister and her venereal playboy husband. He was killed in the war; she committed suicide, her health impaired by the disease she contracted from him that had also affected the body of their daughter.

Trying to show more understanding than his own father ever attempted to, Jerry is confronted with children more rebellious than he was. He has to deal with sexual experiments, drunkenness, an abortion, the Communism of George and Jan, and the Communist leanings and death of Dennis, who is shot while reporting a labor uprising. The younger son, Bill, an initial disappointment, marries Judge Poindexter's daughter, and plans to work in St. Cloud as did Jerry and Jerry's father before him.

The announcement of Janet Poindexter's pregnancy coincides with Jerry's dock-side farewell to George and his Communist wife, Zita, who are off to aid the Loyalists in Spain. Jan is off to New York City to write for the *Daily Worker*.

Bricks without Straw, Charles Norris's tenth and penultimate novel, was greeted with responses even more mixed than *Zelda Marsh* and *Seed.* The most telling reviews were negative. Once again, some of the most favorable reviews came, belatedly, from England. J. O. Beresford of the *Manchester Guardian,* on 14 October 1938, praised especially Jerry Kennedy's wife, Connie, and, regarding the novel as a whole, concluded: "Like earlier of Mr. Norris's novels, this is an honest study of character, somewhat overloaded in the matter of detail but never dull."[11] On the same day, the *London Times* generally concurred with Beresford's judgment. Although the *Times* reviewer found it difficult to determine for what besides "mutual human understanding Norris is crusading, since his sympathies . . . seem as evenly divided as his characters' views . . . ," he was convinced that "the crusader's loss is the novelist's gain." Noting in passing Norris's "rather bald depiction of the disastrous effects of youthful sexual indiscretion," he viewed Jerry Kennedy as a father "much more vividly and likeably alive" than he was as a son and allowed that, although *"Bricks without Straw* will make no history . . . as a leisurely and persuasive story of American manners and men and women it has its definite attraction."[12]

Earlier, on America's own shores, the *Springfield Republican* for 25 September 1938 compared *Bricks without Straw* favorably with Sinclair Lewis's *The Prodigal Parents:* "Not a novel of striking originality but understandably conceived and skillfully managed, and carrying the reader's interest with it . . . a story . . . of the inevitable human elements in the later years of adolescence and the first period of adult life."[13] *Time* for 12 September 1938 first noted that Norris's nine novels had "brought him neither the literary reputation of his brother nor the profits of his wife. But they have been moderately good, moderately successful, have kept him from being known as simply 'Kathleen Norris's husband.'" Then it went on to mildly praise *Bricks without Straw:* "Compared with the jaundiced eyes of [Sinclair] Lewis or the rheumy eyes of Howard Spring, author Norris's eyes seem cool-sighted. His calm view comes . . . of his studied concern always to see both sides of problems. . . ."[14]

Robert Van Gelder and May Lamberton Becker had more mixed views. Writing for the *New York Times Book Review,* on 11 September 1938, Van Gelder predictably saw Norris's style as "lax, thoroughly commonplace." Withal, he continued, "Mr. Norris is objective. He attempts to do justice to all points of view and succeeds fairly well."[15] In the *New York Herald Tribune Books* for 4 September 1938 Becker wrote of Norris's theme of "Parents Against Sons," the "inability of each generation to understand the next." She complained that it had been handled better many times before: "Genius said it in as few words as possible in Turgenev's *Fathers and Sons."* To Becker, it was not

Norris's art but "his solid sympathy" that "has a cumulative effect upon the reader."[16]

The *Saturday Review of Literature,* on 10 September 1938, and the *Christian Science Monitor,* on 21 September 1938, were even less positive. The anonymous author of "Fathers and Sons" for the *Saturday Review* saw in the "tone of [the] final pages [that] Mr. Norris is no more satisfied by the inconclusiveness of it all than is the reader." The reviewer judged that "The whole book is handled without [Norris's] customary assurance." He concluded that the result was "a fumbling and pedestrian book which is unsatisfactory by my standard, and surely most of all by those of Mr. Norris himself."[17] M. W. S. of the *Monitor* declared that "the whole book an extended platitude" in which Norris's "so-called realism seems to serve as a mechanism for disguising what is trite and sentimental in the story."[18] The *New Republic,* on 14 September 1938, summed up its own less than positive reactions to the novel a bit more generously, seeing it as "The battle of the generations described with knowledge and sympathy and no great fire of genius."[19] Only Kenneth Horan of the *Chicago Journal of Commerce* (in one of the blurbs on the novel's dust jacket) held that "This is Charles G. Norris's best book."

Influences

The biographical influences in *Bricks without Straw* are readily apparent. Jerry Kennedy's father is a "leading elder in the First Presbyterian Church,"[20] as was Norris's father. Jerry plays some of the same piano pieces that Charles Norris played for relaxation and for the pleasure of Kathleen when she was bedridden with rheumatism. Both Jerry and his author grieve over the sudden death of a brother and witness the terrible grief of a devoted mother. Laura Kennedy is as devastated over the death of her George as Gertrude Norris was over the death of Lester. The hostility that Charles felt for his father as deserter is translated into Jerry's youthful aversion to Mr. Kennedy as tyrant. He "wanted to be anything except like his father" (32).

Obvious literary borrowings are less apparent than biographical parallels in *Bricks without Straw.* Norris has better integrated passages and echoes from other writers than he was to in his next and last finished novel, *Flint.* Yet he is still using large heroines with "white strong column[s]" (45) for throats, similar to Frank Norris's heroines. Jerry, again in the manner of Ross Wilbur in *Moran,* "had even come to wrestling, he attempting to subdue [Connie] by force" (171–72). Like Frank Norris, Charles objects to the "rat's nest of bohemians," the arty crowd of Greenwich Village. Syphilis plays a deadly role in *Bricks without Straw* as it does in *Vandover,* although Charles is more open about discussing it in 1938 than Frank could afford to be in the 1890s: "In Jerry's day half of the fraternity men on campus had been diseased and had been unashamed of it" (199). One of Jerry's friends (later his brother-in-law) brags about his many bouts with venereal disease. Another friend dies of a single encounter with syphilis, as does Dolly Haight in *Vandover.*

Judgments

Bricks without Straw contains more than a few of Charles Norris's lapses, including the usual spate of clichés or verbal expressions inappropriate to their contexts: "You can lead a horse to water, but you can't make him drink" (44); "The girl is free, white and of age" (307); or the narrator's blatant: "Kelsey . . . believed any girl could be laid . . . ," a remark which trails off into "he had had several affairs with women . . ." (17). Jerry's initial reactions to the news of his unmarried girlfriend's pregnancy are in character: "He sat looking at [Connie], his jaw slightly fallen, thinking first of himself—next both of them—of the trouble in store, the complications ahead" (75). But his subsequent reactions are overdone and overwritten: "somewhere inside of her, life, with which he had impregnated her, was already stirring, and . . . months hence, she would give him a son or a daughter of whom he should be the proud father! His heart grew big, a great breath filled his lungs" (78–79). At a later point, when Jerry expresses rage over his children's communism, what erupts is a pathetic parody of Lear, after hearing of Cordelia's death: "Oh-oh-oh-oh-oh!" (353). The impact of the novel's concluding page is also dissipated by the previously flippant announcement of Janet Poindexter's pregnancy in words that end the novel: "Hello Grandma and Grandpa."

But, as in all but his weakest novels, the stronger passages and Norris's sound sense of structure prevail. Zita Reynolds came immediately alive, as seen through Jerry's exaggerated view: "over her temple a wisp of red hair escaped, suggesting sharp-pointed horns, and in her tight black suit . . . she looked like an incarnate young devil" (273). Norris's description of the St. Cloud professors "with unattractive wives" is cruelly accurate, as is his wry description of the amateur college show that stars Jerry's vain and stage-struck daughter Marianne (294–98). Several of Norris's minor characters haunt the memory: "The Riordan girls—bold hussies with bold eyes and big hips, who wriggled their rumps deliberately when they left or entered a room" (17). He can also register affection in his description of an aesthetically unappealing female body. Jerry "noticed [his wife, Laura's] big hips, her waistline all but gone, her fat arms and fleshy shoulders as she disappeared through the door, and although the vision was not alluring, he was conscious of no distaste, rather of affection and pleasure" (184–85). Norris's description of snow-covered backyards in New York City is fine (6) as are his careful observations of 1920s architecture (186–87). The one sentence describing Jerry's and Connie's unhappy surrender to Mr. Kennedy's wishes is wonderfully understated: "Early in October, Jerry and his wife boarded a train at the Grand Central Station and left for St. Cloud" (89). Another effect featuring ironic juxtaposition externalizes Jerry's stunned condition at the scene of his son George's auto accident. While he looks at the wrecked car (George had been taken to the hospital before his arrival), "Overhead spread the purple canopy of night with its shining pinpoints of light. A cock crowed, a dog barked, and from far away came the first rattle of milk cans" (230).

Norris consistently manages his thematic structural parallels without violating consistency of character. Connie's outburst of frustration at the stifling environs of St. Cloud is prepared for. It also incapsulates the theme of conformity and rebellion that runs throughout the novel (121). Zita's rebellious indifference to the institution of marriage while she is living with George parallels Connie's earlier refusal to marry Jerry (300, 58). Marianne's decision to have an abortion parallels Connie's earlier objection to abortion (on religious grounds) before her miscarriage. Marianne's affair with her young actor who promised them fame in Hollywood is a variation on Connie's submission to the man who financed the first stages of her singing career.

Norris is particularly effective in his management of the near failure of Jerry's bank years after the crash of 1929. Although the novel contains many blatant attacks on the capitalistic system, the picture of Jerry (the leading capitalist of St. Cloud), sitting in his car on Washington's birthday outside a mansion he can no longer afford, is an indelibly moving one (236–37). He contemplates the suicide of his friend-colleague, the revered Lion Halliday, who had recently killed himself in his bath, an act that is prepared for in an earlier newspaper headline that Norris inserts in the manner of John Dos Passos (219). There is a nice ironic touch in a comparable scene: Jan (a closet Communist) sits across the living room from her beloved Uncle Jerry and quietly reads Spengler's *The Decline of the West* while he contemplates what seems to be their inevitable bankruptcy signaled by the failure of his own bank (252–53). *Bricks without Straw* is most effective when Norris sticks to these kinds of dramatic scenes, since confrontations between communism and capitalism are often presented too much as set pieces and are not always well integrated into the texture of the novel.

In the main, however, he handles the issues of drinking, sexual freedom, abortion, marriage versus career, double standards, women's liberation, child/parent relationships, and communism versus capitalism frankly and effectively. The parallels and reversals among the generations clarify human nature rather than obscure it. Norris again strove successfully to present both sides of controversial issues fairly. The 11 August 1945 *Saturday Review* obituary[21] of him includes an anecdote about his giving one of his nieces a hundred-dollar check to write a letter that appears in the novel as Jan's defense of her belief in communism to her Uncle Jerry. Although himself not sympathetic to the Communist cause and not pleased when his niece signed the check over to the Communist party as her "favorite charity," Norris let the letter stand unedited.

Like its author, *Bricks without Straw* has integrity. But, although it is another of Charles G. Norris's eminently readable books, it is too mechanical and too unwieldy to be one of his best. This penultimate novel, too, deserved its mixed reviews.

Flint: Plot and Reactions

Flint focuses on the virtual annihilation of the wealthy ship-owning Rutherford family during the labor/management strife in San Francisco from 1933 to 1938. The principal antagonists are Stan Rutherford, son of J. O. B. and Frances Rutherford, and Rory O'Brien, labor leader and agitator, actually cousin of Stan and son of the prominent lawyer, Lloyd Rutherford and his wife Bessie. Before the novel ends, Stan's playboy cousin, Chris, is dead of tuberculosis; Stan's father is dead of a heart attack prompted by a vicious verbal attack by Rory O'Brien during a bargaining session; and Stan's Uncle Lloyd dies of a heart attack during O'Brien's theft of his own birth certificate.

By the end of the novel, all the Rutherford males are dead, as are two of the Rutherford women. Bessie Rutherford dies from the complications of an operation on her leg, fractured during the mayhem after a man looking like O'Brien (her son) threw a gas bomb into the wedding reception of her daughter Eleanor. Aunt Charmion Baxter (sister of J. O. B. and Lloyd) dies as the result of a labor riot. Vincent Oliver, the first fiancé of Stan's sister, Daisy, is stabbed to death by thugs hired by the dock workers union. And the novel climaxes in Rory's shooting both Stan and his own former mistress, Caddie Welch, as they lie in each other's arms in Caddie's bed. Then Rory shoots himself.

At the novel's conclusion, the only Rutherford survivors (not counting Uncle Reggy Baxter, widower of Charmion) are grandmother Rutherford, who continues to preside over the ever diminishing family at her annual Christmas breakfasts; Daisy, who has recovered from a nervous breakdown and married Syd Watterbury, the new shipping company president; Cousin Eleanor, who has shed her first husband, a narcissistic actor, for a second more worthy husband, Byron Mackey, a brilliant political visionary and labor sympathizer; and Frances Rutherford, Stan's distraught mother.

Although Norris's last novel is more plausible than any summary of it, except for a minority report or two it met either mixed or unfavorable reviews. The most favorable review was Richard A. Cordell's "Assorted Disasters in a Furious Theme" for the *Saturday Review of Literature*, on 8 January 1944.[22] While in his view *Flint* shared with Norris's other novels an "almost complete lack of irony and humor" and the characters were "vaguely realized," he called it "a knock out narrative" that radiates "an underminable power." Cordell saw "The theme in *Flint*" (which he labeled "the internecine conflict between labor and capital") "powerful and genuine. . . . The author presents with scrupulous fairness the claims and grievances of both sides and actually is less romantic than John Steinbeck, Josephine Herbst or Michael Gold in picturing the class struggle. In spite of tedious, sagging passages of debate and analysis, the book illumines rather than preaches, and is thus superior to such earlier thesis novels as *Seed, Bread,* and *Brass.*" Thomas Sugrue, writing for the *New York Times Book Review,* on 9 January 1944, was flippant, but also relatively positive. He concluded: "If you'd like the capital-labor situation served up with a dash of murder and a touch of sex, this is for you." Earlier in his review he acknowledged that "With this complicated set of characters, and with [the] mysterious sub-plot . . . Mr. Norris manages to tell a good yarn. . . ." He objected to Norris's use of "Force" as a dominant character without identifying it with anything: "It is not spiritual, not even in the Luciferian sense. Sprung from . . . material luxuries—it feeds upon the misty notion that all men were born with the right to high wages for short hours—and large profits for small investments. With both sides so deeply wrong . . . it is no wonder that the only solution offered is victory for one of the combatants." Sugrue piously objected to the absence of any "word in favor of a little Christian love to leaven the hearts of all concerned." On the style of *Flint* he added that while Norris "might sharpen his tools" and avoid "clichés" he had written the novel "skillfully."[23]

Booklist for 1 February 1944 labeled *Flint* "the melodramatic story of a shipbuilding family."[24] John Cort, reviewing for *Commonweal,* on 14 April 1944, took a more definite stand: "Mr. Norris has tried to write a novel about class conflict in San Francisco and has failed rather badly." Cort claimed that "Mr.

Norris seems to be one of those who thinks, and rightly so, that a preponderance of justice was on the side of the workers in the San Francisco troubles, at least in the beginning. And yet his weakness for the stolid charm and . . . the amenities of the rich obviously make him incapable of whipping up either intensity or passion over the fate of the underdogs."²⁵ Jennings Rice of the *New York Herald Tribune Weekly Book Review*, on 4 January 1944, made the same astute observation: "Oddly enough, it is in its presentation of labor's side of the story that the book is least convincing. . . . It would have been far more effective dramatically if the reader had been permitted to visit behind the lines with the forces of labor, as he does with the forces of management, and see them in action. . . ." Rice closed by attacking the basic structure of *Flint:* "Lacking adequate preparation both psychological and factual . . . [the] tragic episode with which the story ends . . . bursts on the reader with the noisy emptiness of an operatic thunderclap."²⁶

Borrowings and Steinbeck

Norris again drew from his autobiographic reservoir in the making of *Flint*. Grandmother Rutherford is drawn largely from Gertrude Norris, especially in her "leading roles in amateur theatrics" before her marriage. And like Gertrude Norris's youthful career hopes, "Ambitions of earlier years . . . had been thwarted. . . ."²⁷ Charles and Kathleen Norris had themselves met phony and narcissistic actors like Eleanor's first husband, Lester Armitage neé Emil Gettlesohn, in their own dealings with his studio, Metro-Goldwyn-Mayer. The Rutherfords stay at the Chatham, the Norrises' favorite hotel, a jumping off place for their trip to England for the coronation of King George—a trip that involves preparations like the Norrises' and almost their exact itinerary. Byron Mackey's plan to eliminate such "scandals" as "venereal disease" is a nod in the direction of one of the pet projects of the Norrises' physician, Dr. Russell Lee (330).

Borrowings from Frank Norris are moderately evident. The pistol shots that interrupt Eleanor's wedding reception sound much like those from the barn dance shootout in *The Octopus* (110–11). But the most interesting borrowings are from another novel that Charles Norris had recently read with great care, *The Grapes of Wrath.*

His private judgment of Steinbeck's novel, made clear in a letter to the San Francisco journalist and critic Joseph Henry Jackson (1894–1946), reveals as much about himself as it does about his opinion of *Grapes of Wrath:*

I have waited to answer your nice letter of the sixth until I had finished "Grapes of Wrath." You don't reveal your own reactions to the book and so I feel like walking on tiptoe in describing mine, *but* I think it is one of the finest jobs I've read in a long, long time. He makes me so humble that I feel inclined to quit writing altogether— and just forget I've ever had a book printed. If you want to gather that I am tossing my hat in the air about "G. of W.," you're right. As to the conditions he describes—that's different. Different in so far as this,— that there are world forces on the loose and individuals are being crushed and destroyed and debauched and murdered just as they have always been when world forces—economic ones—get loose. It isn't quite fair—or is it?—to paint the picture of an individual case and arouse your readers' sympathies for that particular case. A million Chinamen are killed or starve—and who cares—particularly? We recognize their plight as the tragic result of the failure of harvests or the aggression of a nation. Our shipowners and our business men right here in San Francisco are being crushed and destroyed and murdered and annihilated by economic forces they cannot control—and you and I feel sorry for them because we happen to know them, they're nice guys, and belong to our Club—but in the long run, what does it matter? I'm thinking of the Crusades and all the people who were killed and who perished as the result of them. Who cares—today? I'm struggling to think—"thinking out loud"; Uncle Tom in "Uncle Tom's Cabin" was a pathetic figure and the book did a lot toward making people fight and remedy a situation the unfairness of which revolted them. Maybe "Grapes of Wrath" will do the same thing.

I hope my feeble effort in writing the book I'm attempting, won't be propaganda in any form—but, oh Jesus!—it is hard to keep the propaganda out of it! I'm tackling a much harder job than Steinbeck— with, as I've already said, one twentieth of his ability.[28]

Since Charles Norris was trying hard to look at both sides of a complex issue—this time the migrant worker/farm owner's struggle—judiciously and "keep the propaganda out of it," he doubtless thought that he *was* "tackling a much harder job than

Steinbeck." Norris continued to find it extremely difficult to present his social and political issues in a balanced manner. Oscar Lewis's praise of Norris's "handling of the labor problem" in a letter to him on 9 February 1944 points out his achievement most perceptively: "I imagine it will please everyone except labor and the shipowners, and if they both object it will mean only that you have held the scales evenly."[29] When the propaganda does creep into his novel, it is usually in the mouths of sympathetic characters on both sides of the management/labor struggle, each of whom has understandably strong convictions. And, while most of the characters in *Flint* are not his most memorable, Norris has in Caddie Welch created not a mere pro-labor apologist but a vibrant woman who in her earthiness, intelligence, and determination suggests a younger Ma Joad. While *Flint* is not Norris's best novel, it was written by a man who not only had considerably more than "one twentieth" the ability of Steinbeck but the good sense to borrow from Steinbeck's most powerful novel and strengthen the matrix of what was to be his own final literary effort.

Although Norris plays variations on Steinbeck's pro-worker theme and tries to look at both sides of the complex struggle with more objectivity than Steinbeck, he follows much of the language in *The Grapes of Wrath* very closely. Steinbeck describes the government facilities at Weedpatch with its "sanitary units"[30] complete with "toilets, and showers and washtubs."[31] Saturday night entertainment in a recreation hall features music (a "strang band") and dancing.[32] One of the deputies hired by the growers to make trouble for the workers is not pleased with the idea of Weedpatch: "Them goddamn gov'ment camps. . . . Give people hot water, an' they gonna want hot water. Give 'em flush toilets, an' they gonna want 'em. . . . You give them goddamn Okies stuff like that a' they'll want 'em. . . . They hol' red meetin's in them gov'ment camps. All figgerin' how to get on relief. . . ."[33] Stan Rutherford's Uncle Reggie Baxter, in a beleaguered condition, expresses views even more cynical than those of Steinbeck's deputy:

"The Government builds camps for them, dozens of 'em, with running water, hot and cold shower baths, recreation halls; they have music, dancing, and movies. Our Country Fair Grounds have been turned into an Okie playground, and naturally the Okies think it's pretty soft. Listen. This year I ran short of cotton pickers, tried my damndest to get some; there were none to be had. Why? Because they are being supported by the Government and didn't want work. By the end of one year they are allowed to vote in this state, and of course they vote for a governor and a legislature who will keep 'em on relief." (160)

Results

Although the Okies do not appear as central characters in *Flint* (as do the dockworkers and labor agitators) they do represent one of two major forces that Norris's novel is largely about: labor versus capitalism. Norris's treatment of this particular illustration of his major theme would not have been the same without the avid and appreciative reading of *Grapes of Wrath* to which his letter to Jackson and his novel to the world are clear testament.

On the debit side of *Flint,* Norris continues to have problems with his use of colloquialisms. Stan sums up his passion for Caddie: "'You—you . . .' he floundered; 'you get my goat,' he finished clumsily" (221). Shortly before O'Brien murders them, Stan says to Caddie: "'You darling! You say "scat" to my blues, and fooey, they're gone!'" (338). Norris's handling of Stan's hostile reaction to O'Brien's picture in Caddie's bedroom also rings false: "There was something malevolent about the man's face, and a strong feeling of disgust rose within him. As he set [the picture] back in its place, a foul word said with venom and hatred escaped him, and he spat on the likeness" (232). Norris's attempts to externalize Stan's conflicts over his sexual temptation are too obvious: "As [Stan] strode along, almost everything he saw reminded him of his struggle: a stalled motorcar with a coughing engine, striving to make headway, a dog straining at the leash held in the hand of a pretty girl, a heavy truck groaning and laboring up a steep incline . . . a bird fluttering at an upstairs window of a house, vainly trying to enter. Conflicts all!" (240).

Although it does, at times, read a bit too much like a soap opera with a gimmicky and predictable ending, *Flint* is well structured, and Norris manages to move his large cast around with considerable grace. Most of the action is unified and the characters remain consistent to their natures. When Stan jealously contemplates climbing five floors and knocking on Caddie's door to find out "if it was locked" (302), he unconsciously foreshadows cousin Rory O'Brien's agitated climb of these same stairs with an ax in his hands and a gun in his pocket. And while the reader does not get to know a single character well enough soon enough, by the time he gets to know Stan, Norris has explored the centers of consciousness of several of the other key characters to good advantage. The personal worlds of Frances (6–7) and Daisy (15–16) provide a backdrop for his more extensive treatment of Stan's thoughts and feelings. Being inside their minds even for so brief a time helps the reader to better empathize with them during their long periods of trial. Once again Norris succeeds with his realistic descriptions, whether it be that of J. O. B.'s house (12–13) or the general strike in San Francisco (58–78) or the coronation of King George (265–67).

But then again the mixed reviews were deserved. For while Charles Norris's eleventh and last published novel does present the opposing forces of labor and capital fair-mindedly, it remains one of his most loquacious efforts. The long set speeches in defense of labor, communism, capitalism, and free enterprise, however intelligent, slow down the action too much. On the other hand, Norris's mingling of the plight of the Rutherford family in San Francisco in the pre–World War II period with talk of Hitler and Mussolini and the coronation of a British king captures the ironic juxtapositions of the decade with the "truth and accuracy" that Frank Norris valued so highly. If *Flint* is not one of Charles Norris's best books, it is one of his most intelligent.

Chapter Seven
Conclusion

As a manipulator of book publishers and magazine editors on whom he so persistently urged his will, Charles G. Norris was a major force in the creation and sustenance of the kind of popular fiction the American reading public consumed for over thirty years. He sold almost a hundred Norris family book manuscripts and over a thousand short stories, articles, columns, movie scripts, and reviews from 1910 to 1945. The vacuum created largely by the absence of his canny knowledge of popular taste and his forceful will has prompted the critical world and reading public to neglect him almost totally for nearly forty years. His books, unlike his brother's and wife's, did not go into paperback editions during his lifetime and were not reprinted after his death.[1] Readers had to seek them out in secondhand book stores and established libraries. Critics who could have read him if they wanted to had other fish to fry. Yet, while he was a wholeheartedly devoted brother and husband, forever championing Frank's and Kathleen's books, he was equally determined as a fellow professional writer in the research and composition of each of his own eleven major efforts.

Charles Norris was not always a good writer; in fact, at times he wrote quite badly. But throughout his eleven very substantial novels integrity and power vibrate. His novels offer an extensive record of middle-class and upper-middle-class life in San Francisco and New York from 1890 to 1940. If Charles Norris is not in the league with such writers he knew and admired as Dreiser, Fitzgerald, and his brother Frank, he remains more important than the Kathleen Norrises, the Fannie Hursts, and the Edna Ferbers. His work fits comfortably in the camp of another of his friends, Sinclair Lewis, whom enough people admired sufficiently to award him the Nobel Prize. Charles Norris remains unduly neglected. Although books like *Salt, Brass,* and *Pig Iron* do not make him a candidate for a Nobel Prize, they are as good as some of Lewis's novels and better than others.

Claims that his writing is essentially humorless, is rarely spectacular, and does not approach greatness have validity. Norris always wrote with difficulty, working slowly and painfully, while his wife breezed through her writing with seeming effortlessness. C. Edmunds Allen sums up the striking differences in their work habits: "Writing for C. G. Norris was hard work. He had a routine he called putting on the hair shirt in which he would go on the wagon, go to an isolated spot and work all day, day after day, until the project was finished. Kathleen, on the other hand, had a routine of writing 5000 words every day after breakfast [leaving the pages on the floor for her secretary to gather up and retype] and quitting for the day."[2] Just as he could not match Kathleen's quick Irish wit in conversation, he lacked the fluidity of style that came to her so easily. Yet however doggedly created, Norris's novels are workmanlike in the best sense and always intelligently rendered and readable. If there is no appreciable artistic development in his writing, the fine quality of his perceptive observations of American life is admirably consistent. His avowed purpose in writing was to make people think. Charles Norris's novels are clearly in the tradition of William Dean Howells, of Frank Norris, and, to a greater degree, of Theodore Dreiser.

At the same time that Hemingway was forging his clean-cut prose, when Joyce was pushing language beyond old boundaries, and Faulkner was experimenting with the very structure of the novel to get at the truth of the human heart, Charles G. Norris was fighting a more modest battle. He was carrying forth many of the less experimental but sturdily traditional aspects of the late nineteenth-century novel. In his concern with exploring economic, political, and, above all, social issues in well-made novels, he has created, from their beginnings and through their struggles to what are, almost inevitably, muted defeats, the lives of characters for whom he cares. He has carried on the spirit of overt political, economic, and social exploration so apparent in Howells's *The Rise of Silas Lapham* and *A Hazard of New Fortunes* and in Frank Norris's last two novels, *The Octopus* and *The Pit*. He has broadened the base of Sinclair Lewis's exposé of the middle-class Midwesterner, the pretentious small-town American that Mencken characterized so trenchantly. While Charles Norris's Samuel Osgood Smith and Philip Baldwin share some of the same superficial values as Lewis's George F. Babbitt and Carol Kennicott, they also share more of their author's sympathy—and with it the reader's. Like Howells's Silas Lapham, they matter.

Charles, like Frank Norris and Dreiser, was not at his best as a systematic thinker. His ambivalent concern for determinism, particularly in his use of the overwhelming power of social and economic forces, was sporadic. He was much more adept at capturing, as Arnold Goldsmith puts it, "the daily problems of real men and women who constantly have to worry about such things as jobs, bills, budgets, birth control and divorce," and examining "such problems as the trapped housewife, the interference of inlaws, and the population explosion."[3]

If his work lacks the emotional impact of the best of Dreiser, his technique of building up detail upon detail is less cumbersome than most of Dreiser. Although he lacked much of his brother's profound capacity for self-irony and ambivalence, he shared Frank Norris's ability to tell a good story. And the well-researched issues that Charles Norris argues both probingly and judiciously always have a realistic context, which lends them credence. He does make people think. And when he is at his best, as in *Salt, Brass,* and *Pig Iron,* his novels have an enviable power. They are well worth seeking out and reading.

Charles G. Norris is significant as a contributing member of a broad literary circle, including Dreiser, Mencken, Lewis, Fitzgerald, and Steinbeck, as well as many of the lesser lights of the first four decades of the century. His books have obvious historical value. His personality was a determining force on a period of popular taste in a critical stage in the evolution of the American novel.

Notes and References

Chapter One

1. Gertrude Glorvina Doggett was born on 20 May 1841 in Mendon, Massachusetts.
2. Grace and Flora both died before they were a year old.
3. The name Carlton Booth Norris was written on the birth certificate.
4. They were married in Chicago, Illinois, on 27 May 1867.
5. See Charles G. Norris, *Frank Norris, 1870–1902: An intimate sketch of the man who was universally acclaimed the greatest American writer of his generation* (New York, 1914), p. 2.
6. Ibid., p. 4.
7. Ibid., p. 8.
8. See the Charles Norris collection at the Bancroft Library, University of California at Berkeley; this collection hereafter cited as Bancroft Library.
9. Charles Norris's official transcript is available in the Records Archives, University of California at Berkeley.
10. Kathleen Norris, *Family Gathering* (Garden City, N.Y., 1959), pp. 86–87.
11. In a letter to Richard Allan Davison, 26 August 1981.
12. Kathleen Norris, *Family Gathering,* p. 75.
13. Ibid., p. 83.
14. Ibid., p. 98.
15. Bancroft Library.
16. Ibid.
17. It is well known among Norris's family and his intimates that he used his influence to get younger talented writers jobs with various publishing companies, magazines and newspapers.
18. Bancroft collection.
19. Ibid.
20. Contracts for all of Charles Norris's novels are in the possession of his son, Dr. Frank Norris.
21. Kathleen Norris, *Family Gathering,* p. 147.
22. Charles and Kathleen exchanged frequent letters during the eighteen months he was at Madison Barracks and Camp Dix.
23. Charles Norris's correspondence to F. Scott Fitzgerald is in the Firestone Library at Princeton University.
24. Kathleen Norris, *Family Gathering,* p. 164.

25. Both letters are in the Bancroft Library.
26. From the author's interview with Dr. Lee on 10 June 1979.
27. Dobie, "Frank Norris, or, Up from Culture," *American Mercury* 13 (April 1928): 412–24.
28. All of the correspondence with Charles Caldwell Dobie referred to is in the Bancroft Library.
29. One of many tributes to Norris's genius for business comes from C. Edmunds Allen: "C. G.'s business acumen was not limited to the literary business. After the crash of 1929, the brokerage house with which he did business failed and the probability was that all would be lost. He hired Morris Ernst, who was later to become one of the most prominent literary and theatrical attorneys. . . . Ernst told me that Norris's vigor and financial understanding along with his own . . . legal ability brought the Norrises through not unscathed but only modestly damaged." See footnote 17.
30. Kathleen Norris, *Family Gathering*, pp. 213–14.
31. Bancroft Library.
32. The Norris/Walker correspondence is in the Bancroft Library.
33. In conversation with Mrs. Frank Norris and in a letter from her of 28 April 1980.
34. The Rinehart/Norris correspondence is in the possession of Dr. Frank Norris.
35. Kathleen Norris, *Family Gathering*, pp. 232–34.
36. Ibid., p. 268.
37. In the possession of Dr. Norris.
38. Bancroft Library.
39. From the author's interview with the late Mrs. Dawson on 1 January 1980.
40. From a 16 August 1981 letter to the author.
41. In the possession of Dr. Norris.
42. Bancroft Library.
43. Kathleen Norris, *Family Gathering*, p. 280.
44. *Noon: An Autobiographical Sketch* (Garden City, N.Y., 1925), p. 82.
45. Kathleen Norris, *Family Gathering*, p. 211.
46. In the possession of Mrs. Hartley Cravens.

Chapter Two

1. Charles G. Norris, *The Amateur* (New York, 1916), pp. 147–48; hereafter page references cited in the text.
2. Bancroft Library.

3. Wilson Follett, review of *The Amateur* in the *Atlantic Monthly* 118 (October 1916):499.
4. Review of *The Amateur* in the *New York Times Book Review*, 12 March 1916, p. 82.
5. E. F. E., "A Young American's Battle with Life," *Boston Evening Transcript*, 11 March 1916, p. 8.
6. Review of *The Amateur*, "Recent Fiction," *Literary Digest* (1 April 1916), p. 910.
7. Review of *The Amateur* in the *London Evening Standard*, 25 August 1920. See Bancroft collection.
8. Review of *The Amateur* in the *Times Literary Supplement*, 19 August 1920. See Bancroft collection.
9. Review of *The Amateur* in the *Observer*, 5 September 1920. See Bancroft collection.
10. Charles G. Norris, *Salt, or the Education of Griffith Adams* (New York, 1918), pp. 3–4; hereafter page references cited in the text.
11. From a clipping in Charles and Kathleen Norris's scrapbook in the Bancroft Library.
12. Review of *Salt* in the *New York Times Book Review*, 16 June 1918, p. 278.
13. E. F. E., "The Education of a Young American," *Boston Evening Transcript*, 19 June 1918, p. 6.
14. D. K., "Anybody's Biography—Almost," *New York Call*, 14 July 1918, p. 11.
15. Review of *Salt*, "Man's Failure," *Springfield Sunday Republican*, 14 August 1918, p. 15.
16. H. J. L., "Books and Things," *New Republic*, 17 August 1918, p. 80.
17. H. W. Boynton, "Paths and Goals: Five American Novels," *Bookman* 47 (1918):679–80.
18. Review of *Salt* in the *Dial*, 19 September 1918, p. 223.
19. Review of *Salt* in *Publisher's Weekly*, 17 August 1918, p. 556.
20. F. Scott Fitzgerald, "Poor Old Marriage," *Bookman* 59 (1921):253–54. For a fuller discussion of the Norris/Fitzgerald relationship see my "F. Scott Fitzgerald and Charles G. Norris," *Journal of Modern Literature* 10, no.1 (1983)
21. Andrew Turnbull, ed., *The Letters of F. Scott Fitzgerald* (New York: Scribners, 1963), p. 173.
22. Fitzgerald's scrapbook, Firestone Library.
23. Fitzgerald Collection, Firestone Library.
24. Both telegrams are in Fitzgerald's scrapbook at the Firestone.
25. Matthew J. Bruccoli and Jennifer Atkinson, eds., *As Ever, Scott Fitz—* (Philadelphia: Lippincott, 1972), p. 45.

26. F. Scott Fitzgerald's "Bernice Bobs Her Hair" is part of the "Volume of Short Stories," in *Flappers and Philosophers* (New York: Scribners, 1920).
27. Fitzgerald was hard at work on his second novel, *The Beautiful and Damned.*
28. Fitzgerald Collection, Firestone Library.
29. *A Man's Woman* (1900), Frank Norris's fourth novel, is generally considered to be his weakest.
30. George Sterling (1869–1926) was a well known San Francisco poet.
31. Guy J. Forgue, ed., *Letters of H. L. Mencken* (New York: Knopf, 1961), p. 229.
32. Bruccoli and Atkinson: *As Ever, Scott Fitz—*, p. 9.
33. Turnbull, *Letters of F. Scott Fitzgerald*, p. 144.
34. Charles G. Norris, "My Favorite Character in Fiction," *Bookman*, 62 (1925):410.
35. *The Short Stories of F. Scott Fitzgerald*, ed. Malcolm Cowley (New York: Scribners, 1951), pp. 98–99.
36. Bancroft Library.

Chapter Three

1. Interview with Charles and Kathleen Norris, "The Norrises Discuss Marriage," *New York Times Book Review*, 12 March 1922, p. 17.
 2. Estelle Lawton Lindsey, "Kathleen Norris Advises Authors." From Charles and Kathleen Norris's scrapbook, Bancroft Library.
 3. Edwin Francis Edgett, "In His Latest Novel Charles G. Norris Describes the Experiences of More than One Luckless Couple Within the Bonds of Marriage," *Boston Evening Transcript*, 24 August 1921, p. 6.
 4. Louise Maunsell Field, "Should Divorce Be Abolished?" *New York Times Book Review*," 25 September 1921, p. 20.
 5. Review of *Brass*, "Matrimonial Misfits," *Literary Digest*, 29 October 1921, pp. 46–48.
 6. Review of *Brass*, "Briefer Mention," *Dial*, 71 (1921):610.
 7. In Charles and Kathleen Norris's scrapbook, Bancroft Library.
 8. Ibid.
 9. Ibid.; two copies.
10. In Charles and Kathleen Norris's scrapbook, Bancroft Library.
11. Ibid.

12. Ibid.
13. Ibid.
14. Fitzgerald, "Poor Old Marriage," p. 254.
15. In Charles and Kathleen Norris's scrapbook, Bancroft Library.
16. Ibid.
17. Ibid.
18. Bancroft Library.
19. Ibid.
20. H. L. Mencken, review of *Brass* in *Smart Set,* October 1921, p. 141.
21. In Charles and Kathleen Norris's scrapbook, Bancroft Library.
22. Ibid.
23. Fitzgerald Collection, Firestone Library.
24. Charles G. Norris, *Brass, A Novel of Marriage* (New York, 1921), pp. 372–77; hereafter page references cited in the text.
25. Frank Norris, *The Octopus* (Garden City, N.Y.: Doubleday, 1928) II: 26.
26. Frank Norris, *McTeague* (Garden City, N.Y.: Doubleday, 1928), p. 142.
27. F. Scott Fitzgerald, *The Crack Up* (New York: New Directions, 1945), p. 33.
28. Bancroft Library.
29. Fitzgerald, "Poor Old Marriage," p. 254.
30. Bancroft Library.
31. Ibid.
32. Review of *Brass* in the *New York Sun,* 10 September 1921. In Charles and Kathleen Norris's scrapbook, Bancroft Library.
33. Ibid.
34. Ibid.
35. Unidentified review in Charles and Kathleen Norris's scrapbook, Bancroft Library.
36. Review of *Bread* in the *New York Times Book Review,* 19 August 1923, p. 18.
37. Review of *Bread* in *Booklist* 20 (23 December 1923):102.
38. Edwin Francis Edgett, "Woman in the Office and the Home," *Boston Evening Transcript,* 18 August 1923, p. 4.
39. Isabel Paterson, "Mr. Norris's *Bread,*" *New York Tribune News and Review,* 19 August 1923, pp. 17–18.
40. Robert Morss Lovett, "Bread without Yeast," *New Republic* 36 (29 August 1923):23.

41. Louise Maunsell Field, "When Business Is at Odds with Matrimony," *Literary Digest* 1 (23 September 1923):54.
42. H. M. Boynton, "More or Less Realism," *Independent* 3852 (29 September 1923):142.
43. Review of *Bread*, "The Woman in Business," *Springfield Sunday Republican*, 14 October 1923, p. 7a.
44. Review of *Bread*, "Briefer Mention," *Dial* 75 (28 November 1923):507.
45. Review of *Bread*, "A Novel That Marks a Reaction from Feminism," *Current Opinion* 75 (October 1923):433.
46. Review of *Bread*, "Books in Brief," *Nation* 117 (October 1923):410.
47. Ruth Snyder, "Life as It Is Lived in the Social Plight. The New Work of Charles Norris Is Devoted to the Woman in Business," *New York World*, 7 October 1923, p. 11e.
48. Paterson, "Mr. Norris's Bread," pp. 17–18.
49. Field, "When Business Is at Odds with Matrimony," p. 55.
50. *New York Times*, p. 18.
51. Charles G. Norris, *Bread* (New York, 1923), p. 287; hereafter page references cited in the text.
52. Frank Norris, *The Pit* (Garden City, N.Y.: Doubleday, 1928), p. 288.
53. Bancroft Library.

Chapter Four

1. Robert Morss Lovett, "Fiction Notes," *New Republic*, 21 April 1926, p. 50.
2. Review of *Pig Iron* in *Booklist*, 23 June 1926, p. 378.
3. Joseph Wood Krutch, "Work and Win," *Saturday Review of Literature* 2 (6 March 1926):602.
4. Review of *Pig Iron* in *American Mercury* 7 (April 1926):507.
5. Stuart Sherman, "Charles Norris," *New York Herald Tribune Books*, 14 March 1926, p. 1.
6. F. F. K., "In This Month's Fiction Library," *Literary Digest* 4 (April 1926):328.
7. Review of *Pig Iron*, "Novels in Brief," *Nation and Athenaeum* 39 (4 September 1926):650.
8. Review of *Pig Iron*, "New Novels," *London Times Literary Supplement*, 26 August 1926, p. 562.
9. Review of *Pig Iron*, "Briefer Mention," *Dial* 81 (October 1926):352.
10. Francis Edwin Edgett, "An American Youth on the Ladder," *Boston Evening Transcript*, 6 March 1926, p. 4.

11. John W. Crawford, "Norris Portrays the Steel Age," *New York World,* 7 March 1926, p. 6M. The subtitle is "An Evangelical Realist Enlists on the Side of Rebel Angels—His *Pig Iron* Sincere."
12. Charles G. Norris, *Pig Iron* (New York, 1925), p. 2; hereafter page references cited in the text.
13. See note 11.
14. Charles G. Norris, *Zelda Marsh* (New York, 1927), p. 5; hereafter page references cited in the text.
15. Edwin Clark, "Mr. Norris in *Zelda Marsh* Rewrites the Tale of Cinderella," *New York Times Book Review,* 14 August 1927, p. 2.
16. Ruth Burr Sanborn, "Fortune Rules All," *New York Herald Tribune,* 28 August 1927, p. 7.
17. Ernest Southerland Bates, "Love and Lust," *Saturday Review of Literature* 4 (17 September 1927):115.
18. Review of *Zelda Marsh,* "Books in Brief," *Nation* 125 (2 November 1927):484.
19. Edwin Clark's review of *Zelda Marsh* in *Commonweal* 7 (7 December 1927):796.

Chapter Five

1. Review of *Seed,* "The New Books," *Saturday Review of Literature* 7 (September 1930):109.
2. Review of *Seed,* "Books in Brief," *Nation* 131 (27 August 1930):228.
3. V. S. Pritchett, "Love Among the Authors," *Spectator,* 20 December 1930, p. 990.
4. Joseph McSortey, "New Books," *Catholic World* 132 (October 1930):115–16.
5. Alan Reynolds Thomson's review of *Seed* in *Bookman* 72 (September 1930):70.
6. Mary Ross, "Case Histories of Birth Control," *New York Herald Tribune Books,* 17 August 1930, p. 3.
7. Fanny Butcher's review of *Seed* in *Chicago Daily Tribune,* 23 August 1930, p. 12.
8. Horace Gregory, "Norris's Novel Essays Problem of Birth Control," *New York Evening Post,* 16 August 1930, p. 5.
9. Review of *Seed,* "Charles Norris's 'Novel of Birth Control,'" *Springfield Sunday Union,* 14 September 1930, p. 7.
10. John Chamberlain, "Mr. Norris Wrestles with a Social Problem," *New York Times Book Review,* 17 August 1930, p. 7.

11. Harry Hanson, "The First Reader," *New York World,* 14 August 1930, p. 9.
12. Charles G. Norris, *Seed: A Novel of Birth Control* (Garden City, N.Y., 1930), p. 72; hereafter page references cited in the text.
13. Dreiser's 20 October 1930 letter to Charles Norris concerning *Seed* is in the Bancroft Library.
14. George Dangerfield, "Loud with Warning," *Saturday Review of Literature* 9 (20 May 1933):605.
15. Review of *Zest* in *Times Literary Supplement,* 29 August 1933, p. 444.
16. Mary Ross, "The Emotional Life of an Average American," *New York Herald Tribune Books,* 21 May 1933, p. 3.
17. Review of *Zest,* "Seven Women," *New York Times Book Review,* 21 May 1933, p. 6.
18. Review of *Zest,* "Briefer Mention," *Commonweal,* 11 August 1933, p. 374.
19. J. S.'s review of *Zest* in *Canadian Forum* 13 (September 1933):477.
20. Charles G. Norris, *Zest* (Garden City, N.Y., 1933), p. 20; hereafter page references cited in the text.

Chapter Six

1. Max Miller, "Family Circle," *Saturday Review of Literature* 12 (22 October 1935):14.
2. M. W. S., "California Saga," *Christian Science Monitor,* 22 October 1935, p. 18.
3. Stanley Young, "Charles G. Norris's Family Circle," *New York Times Book Review,* 20 October 1935, p. 6.
4. Review of *Hands,* "Shirtsleeves to Shirtsleeves Is Theme of C. G. Norris," *Chicago Tribune,* 25 October 1935, p. 15.
5. Peter Quenell, "New Novels," *New Statesman* 11 (25 January 1936):118.
6. W. E. H., "Charles Norris Takes Up the Theme of 'Short-sleeves-to-Shirtsleeves,'" *Boston Evening Transcript,* 2 November 1935, p. 4.
7. Review of *Hands,* "Hands: Norris's Story of Wealth and Manual Labor," *Springfield Sunday Union and Republican,* 22 December 1935, p. 7e.
8. Herschel Brickell, "Further Additions of Current Books of Unusual Merit," *New York Post,* 7 December 1935, p. 7.
9. Mary Ross, "The American Saga and the Morals of Sweat," *New York Herald Tribune Books,* 20 October 1935, p. 5.

10. Charles G. Norris, *Hands* (New York, 1935), pp. 38, 395; hereafter page references cited in the text.
11. J. O. Beresford, "Realism and Romance," *Manchester Guardian,* 14 October 1938, p. 6.
12. Review of *Bricks without Straw* in the *London Times Literary Supplement,* 14 October 1938, p. 697.
13. Review, "The Generations: Charles G. Norris's 'Bricks without Straw,'" *Springfield Republican,* 25 September 1938, p. 7e.
14. Review of *Bricks without Straw* in *Time* 32 (12 September 1938):70.
15. Robert Van Gelder, "The Young Revolt," *New York Times Book Review,* 11 September 1938, p. 7.
16. May Lamberton Becker, "Parents Against Sons," *New York Herald Tribune,* 4 September 1938, p. 2.
17. Review of *Bricks without Straw,* "Fathers and Sons," *Saturday Review of Literature* 18 (10 September 1938):19.
18. M. W. S., "Literary Norris Dam," *Christian Science Monitor,* 21 September 1938, p. 10.
19. Review of *Bricks without Straw* in the *New Republic* 96 (14 September 1938):168.
20. Charles G. Norris, *Bricks without Straw* (New York, 1938), p. 4; hereafter page references cited in the text.
21. Obituary, *Saturday Review of Literature,* 28 (11 August 1945):20.
22. Richard A. Cordell, "Assorted Disasters in a Furious Theme," *Saturday Review of Literature* 27 (8 January 1944):18.
23. Thomas Sugrue, "Baffled Business Men," *New York Times Book Review,* 9 January 1944, p. 4.
24. Review of *Flint* in *Booklist* 40 (1 February 1944):198.
25. John Cort's review of *Flint* in *Commonweal* 39 (14 April 1944):660.
26. Jennings Rice, "Novels Begin the Year," *New York Herald Tribune Weekly Book Review,* 4 January 1944, p. 6.
27. Charles G. Norris, *Flint* (Garden City, N.Y., 1944), p. 5; hereafter page references cited in the text.
28. Bancroft Library. For a fuller discussion see my "Charles G. Norris and John Steinbeck: Two More Tributes to *The Grapes of Wrath*," *Steinbeck Quarterly* 15 (Summer–Fall 1982):90–97.
29. Ibid.
30. John Steinbeck, *The Grapes of Wrath* (New York: Viking, 1939), p. 391.
31. Ibid., p. 390.
32. Ibid., p. 406.
33. Ibid., p. 445.

Chapter Seven

1. The happy exception is the recent publication of *Salt,* ed. Matthew J. Bruccoli, Lost American Fiction Series (Carbondale: Southern Illinois University Press, 1981).
2. From a letter to the author, 26 August 1981.
3. Arnold Goldsmith, "Charles and Frank Norris," *Western American Literature* 2, no. 1 (Spring 1967):31, 40.

Selected Bibliography

PRIMARY SOURCES

1. Novels
The Amateur. New York: Dutton, 1916; London: Constable, 1920.
Brass: A Novel of Marriage. New York: Dutton, 1918; London: Constable, 1920.
Bread. New York: Dutton, 1923.
Bricks without Straw. Garden City: Doubleday, Doran; London: Heinemann, 1938.
Flint. Garden City: Doubleday, Doran, 1944; London: Hammond, Hammond, 1946.
Hands. New York: Farrar & Rhinehart, 1935; London: Heinemann, 1936.
Pig Iron. New York: Dutton, 1925. London: Murray, 1926.
Salt: Or The Education of Griffith Adams. New York: Dutton, 1918; London: Constable, 1920; reprint. Carbondale, Ill.: Southern Illinois University Press, 1981.
Seed. Garden City: Doubleday, Doran; London: Heinemann, 1930.
Zelda Marsh. New York: Dutton, 1927; London: Harrap, 1928.
Zest. Garden City: Doubleday, Doran, 1933; London: Heinemann, 1938.

2. Biography
Frank Norris. New York: Doubleday, Page, 1914.

3. Plays
A Gest of Robin Hood. San Francisco: Bohemian Club, 1914.
Ivanhoe. San Francisco: Bohemian Club, 1936.
The Rout of the Philistines. San Francisco: Bohemian Club, 1922.

SECONDARY SOURCES

1. Books and Manuscripts
Norris, Kathleen. "An Interview with Kathleen Norris." A series of unpublished interviews with Kathleen Norris conducted in

March 1956 and September 1957, in the Bancroft Library, University of California at Berkeley.
————. *Family Gathering, The Memoirs of Kathleen Norris*. Garden City, N.Y.: Doubleday & Co., 1959. Although occasionally unreliable, the best published source on Charles G. Norris.
————. *Noon: An Autobiographical Sketch*. Garden City, N.Y.: Doubleday, Page, 1925. Useful for the early years of Charles and Kathleen Norris's marriage.
Walker, Franklin. *Frank Norris: A Biography*. Garden City, N.Y.: Doubleday, Doran, 1932; reprint. New York: Russell & Russell, 1963. Still the only biography of Frank Norris.

Most of the unpublished Charles G. Norris material that is not in the possession of family and friends is at the Bancroft Library.

2. Reviews and Articles
    This section does not include the bulk of the contemporary reviews. These can be found in relevant sections of the individual chapters and in the Notes and References to them.
Butcher, Fanny. "*Seed*, by Charles G. Norris." *Chicago Daily Tribune*, 23 August 1930, p. 12. Wrongheaded objection to what she sees as Norris's propaganda in *Seed*.
Chamberlain, John. "Mr. Norris Wrestles with a Social Problem." *New York Times Book Review*, 17 August 1930, p. 7. Sound review praising Norris's knowledge and honesty in *Seed*, but objecting to "too much environmental detail."
Fitzgerald, F. Scott. "Poor Old Marriage." *Bookman* 59 (November 1921):253–54. A perceptive review that tends to underrate *Salt*.
Goldsmith, Arnold L. "*Charles and Frank Norris*." *Western American Literature* 2 (Spring 1967):30–49. The best article on the novels of Charles G. Norris.
Krutch, Joseph Wood. "Work and Win." *Saturday Review of Literature* 2 (6 March 1926):602. Favorable toward *Pig Iron* with just praise of Norris's "dogged seriousness of mind."
Lovett, Robert Morss. "Bread Without Yeast." *New Republic* 36 (29 August 1923):23. A generally perceptive review that spends too much time on Norris's alleged mishandling of salaries in *Bread*.
Mencken, H. L. "Notes on Books." *Smart Set* 66 (October 1921):140–42. Favorable review of *Brass*, lumping Norris's novel with those of Tarkington and Hecht.
Quennell, Peter. *New Statesman and Nation* 11 (25 January, 1936):118. Praises the "extremely interesting picture of social change" in *Hands*.

Index

Ross, Mary, 94, 104, 113, 116
Roth, Herbert, 20

St. Paul News, 59
Sanborn, Ruth Burr, 86
San Francisco Examiner, 9
Saturday Evening Post, 11
Saturday Review of Literature, 33,
    77, 86, 93-94, 103, 112, 120,
    123, 125
Schopenhauer, Arthur, 68
Shaw, George Bernard: *Back to
    Methuselah,* 61
Sherman, Stuart, 78
Siddall, John, 9-10
Sinclair, Upton, 69, 95
Smart Set, 46
Smith, Charles Gilman, 1
Snyder, Ruth, 69
Sox, Harold C., 31, 32
Spectator, 94
Spengler, Oswald: *The Decline of
    the West,* 123
Spring, Howard, 119
*Springfield Sunday Union and
    Republican,* 43, 54, 69, 95,
    113 119
Stassen, Harold, 34
Steinbeck, John, 125, 128, 133;
    The Grapes of Wrath, 127-29
Stowe, Harriet Beecher: *Uncle
    Tom's Cabin,* 127
Sugrue, Thomas, 125
Sunset Magazine, 8

Taft, Robert, 28
Tarbell, Ida M., 9
Thompson, Alan Reynolds, 94
Thompson, David (nephew), 27

Thompson, Francis, 9
Thompson, James
    (brother-in-law), 25
Thompson, James Alden
    (father-in-law), 16, 79
Thompson, Jane (niece), 27
Thompson, Joseph
    (brother-in-law), 16
Thompson, Joseph Jr.,
    (nephew), 27
Tompkins, Juliet Wilbur, 10, 13
Towne, Charles Hansen, 10
Travers, Reginald, 20
Turgenev, Ivan: *Fathers and
    Sons,* 119

Vance, Arthur T., 60
Van Gelder, Robert, 119

Wagner, Richard: *Parsifal,* 71
Walker, Franklin, 12, 13-14,
    22-23
Walton, Harriet (grandmother),
    2, 49
Warren, Earl, 27
Wave, 71
Waxman, Percy, 29
Welles, Orson, 83
Wells, H.G.: *Marriage,* 56, 57;
    Outline of History, 61
Wharton, Edith, 112
Willkie, Wendell Lewis, 28, 34
Wilson, Lois, 22
Woman's Home Companion, 30
Woollcott, Alexander, 22
Wylie, Elinor, 10

Young, Stanley, 112

Zola, Emil, 68, 78, 95, 104